Citroën 2CV

PHOTOGRAPHY DAVID SPARROW
ADRIENNE KESSEL

Grange
BOOKS

Published by Grange Books
An imprint of Books & Toys Ltd
The Grange
Grange Yard
London SE1 3AG

Produced by
Bison Books Ltd
Kimbolton House
117A Fulham Road
London SW3 6RL

ISBN 1-85627-290-7

Printed in Spain by Cayfosa, Barcelona

Page 1: A 2CV of the fifties in a nineties colour.

Pages 2-3: Two white Ducks.

Below: The first concession to fashion – the upholstery is scotch blue.

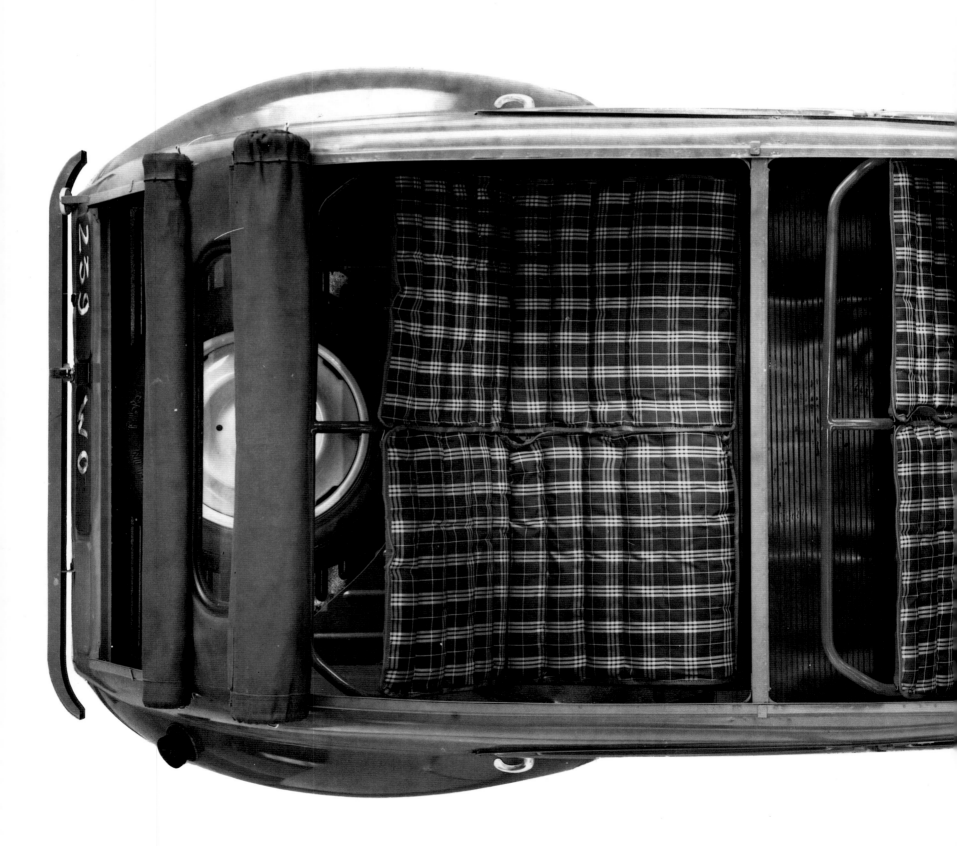

Contents

Introduction

Over 40 years ago, a small car bearing the distinctive Citroën chevrons was introduced to the public in a reserved manner. In those days the Citroën logo was a discreet blue and yellow, and the 1948 brochure was understated; it comprised four 9 × 13cm pages printed in sepia. The 35 lines of text were illustrated by four pictures. It was designed by Marcel Trabaud, who worked in Nice, and was responsible for Citroën's publicity at the time. It was all that was necessary. There would soon be a long waiting list for the new Deux Chevaux; there was nothing to be gained by going over the top.

Left: Citroën's special colour schemes have inspired some owners to create their own versions.

Above: A beautifully restored 1972 2CV4 beneath the Dom Tower in Utrecht; in both Holland and England, 2CVs are more often found in towns and cities than in the country.

Right: In France, the reverse is true; from the chilly plains of the Pas de Calais to the rolling hills of Provence, 2CVs are to be found working in the countryside.

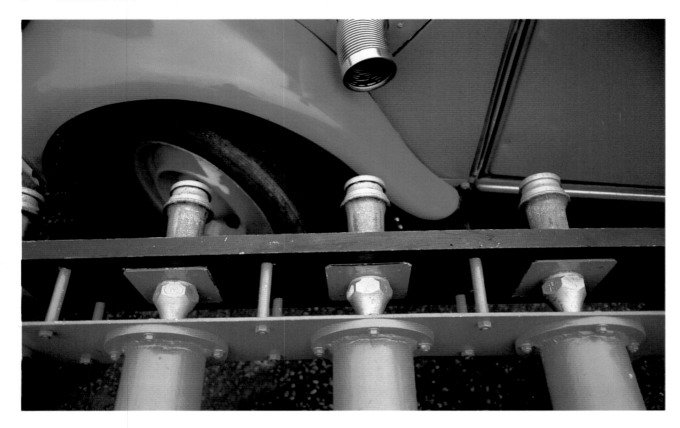

Left: A Duck to water – in this case the hydrants in a fire station; the chrome pipes are mainly for styling purposes – but they serve a practical purpose too as vents to remove the hot-air from the engine compartment.

Below: One of the last of the line; this Portugal-produced 2CV6 Spécial was imported into Holland in July 1990. In smart black, they rolled off the production lines only when there were sufficient orders on the books for a batch to be made.

Right: No shy retiring country girl this, but a Parisienne beauty with unique coachwork by Daniel Girod. Built on a shortened 2CV chassis, she sports bright blue paintwork with chrome trim, including her own 'lady' on her bonnet.

Left: The chevrons on the grille have changed several times in both style and position over the years. The original oval surround disappeared in 1955. Ten years later, the chevrons became smaller and moved up on to the newer-style bonnet. In 1974 they were back on the grille – this time incorporated into the plastic moulding which sat slightly higher on the bonnet than previously.

Right: The Delage red and black Charleston was the original and most popular of the three colour versions. As a result of the extended production life of what was originally a limited edition, hybrids abound. So there are cars with square headlamps and cars with round ones. Round headlamps with red casings or black casings; square headlamps likewise. Red window surrounds and black ones. Black and white seats and quilted grey ones. Perhaps every example is unique after all!

Below left: 'Little Miss Muffett' – an English 2CV definitely not for the arachnophobic. If the large hairy spiders aren't enough, the noise from those air horns should frighten anyone away! There seems to be no limit to the artistic abilities of 2CV owners; cars are decorated with style and charm, wit and imagination.

Below right: A Duck and its owner, in this case Henk van Wezel, an orchestral conductor from Gouda. Boot extension boxes such as this are very popular in Holland but rarely seen elsewhere.

Of Men and Machines

It was partly the company's progressive approach to advertising and marketing which ensured that, by the early 1920s, the Société André Citroën advertised his company and products in the national press. On the first morning of the 7th Paris Motor Show in 1922, Paris awoke to find that the word 'Citroën' had been written in the sky in smoke by an aeroplane. That same year road signs were put up in France, 150,000 of which were stamped with the double chevron logo. The first crossing of the Sahara desert by car took place. Citroën vehicles were dispatched to the most inhospitable of environments to prove their mettle, most famously with the Croisière Noire rally across Africa in 1924 and Croisière Jaune to Peking in 1931. Citroën merchandise included model cars, construction games, a working pedal car called Citroënette, and photo albums. In 1926 factory tours were introduced, the visitors' understanding being enhanced by a scale model of the plant 15 metres long. From 1928 to 1931, readers of the national papers were kept up to date on progress in the Citroën factories. The most famous advertising exploit marked the opening of the International Decorative Arts Exhibition in 1925, when the Eiffel Tower was lit up by a quarter of a million light bulbs forming the Citroën name. Charles Lindbergh claimed to have been guided by them when returning from his solo Atlantic crossing. Despite the extravagance of these ideas, they accounted for only two percent of Citroën's total advertising budget, and also provided the more mundane leaflets, brochures, posters, press releases and showroom material.

André Citroën was born in 1878, the son of a Jewish diamond merchant from Holland who had started in business in Paris. When André first set up his business, it was to manufacture gearwheels; their double helical design was the inspiration for the double chevron device. Called up for war service in 1914, Citroën was soon impressing officials with his plans for the mass-production of shells, which were in seriously short supply. With government backing for the project, he was soon the owner of a very large shell-producing factory in Paris. When the war ended, he decided to turn his hand, and his factory, to producing motor cars. Citroën's forte was in setting up mass production methods that were efficient and cost effective. His cars were reasonably priced, but included as standard such refinements as electric lights, which would have been extras on other marques at that time.

In 1932, at the Paris Salon, Citroën unveiled his new model, the Rosalie. In this year too, the Société des Transports André Citroën, which grew from the taxi company that Citroën had set up in 1923, using his own vehicles, started running a comprehensive bus service throughout France. The double chevrons passed through villages where the horse and cart reigned supreme as private transport, through communities where the concept of owning a

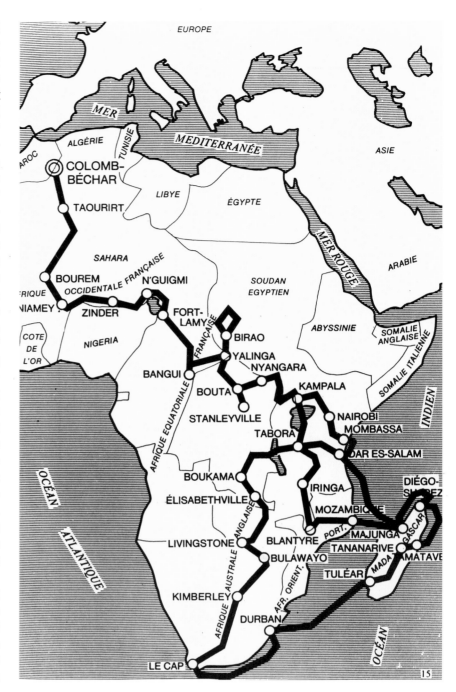

Previous pages: The Traction Avant was unveiled at the Paris Salon in 1934.

Left: André Citroën, 1878-1935.

Above: The route of the Croisière Noire, which took place in 1924. This was the first crossing of the African continent by car, from Colomb-Bechar to the rallying point at Tananarivo, the cars covering a total distance of 20,000 kilometres.

Above right: A Citroën B2, participating in the Croisière Noire, crosses the Great Ruaha River on its way to Lake Nyasa.

Right: André Citroën puts one of his first half-track vehicles through its paces. Sometimes called Kegresse, they were designed by the former chief mechanic to the Tsar of Russia.

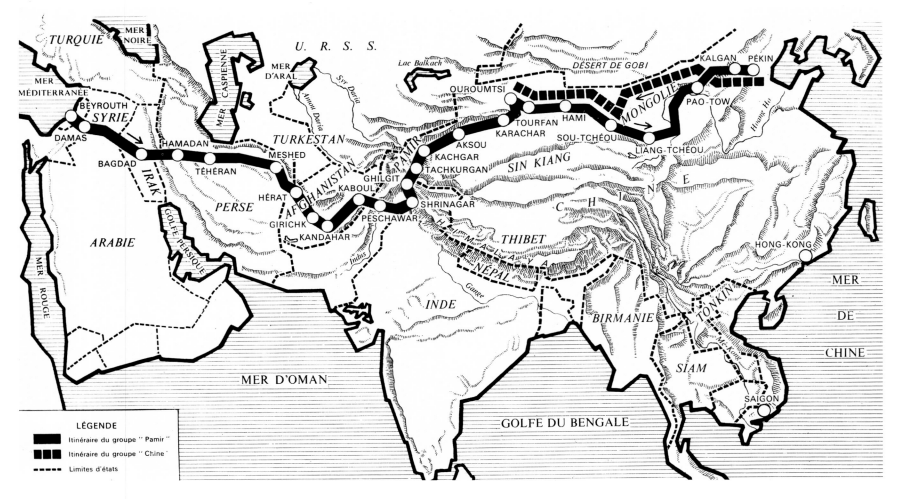

Above: The route of the Croisière Jaune, 1931-32. The map shows two routes: one group of cars started from Beirut, the other from Peking.

Left: The Croisière Jaune took the vehicles across some very rough terrain.

Above right: Leading members of the 2CV team had previously worked on the Traction Avant, including Lefebvre and Bertoni. Although early production was beset with technical and financial problems, this new 7CV Citroën made an immediate impact; between the press launch in the spring of 1934 and its appearance at the Salon in October, over 20,000 were sold. Sadly, André Citroën's success with this model failed to stave off his company's financial ruin. Production of the Traction Avant was to continue until 1957 with no major changes to the design.

car was, for the time being at least, beyond the imagination and means of most people.

With the dawn of a new decade, André Citroën conceived the idea of an inexpensive, stylish car with all possible advantages. He hired new designers and engaged freelance consultants for the project, which was codenamed 'PV' (petite voiture). To take charge, Citroën chose André Lefebvre, whose career had started in aviation at Sup-Aéro. He then went to work for Gabriel Voisin, car-builder extraordinaire, becoming his most brilliant and trusted engineer. In 1923 he raced one of Voisin's cars at the Grand Prix in Monza. He also took part in Voisin's later world-record attempts. Voisin had a friend and rival in Ettore Bugatti, whose curvaceous cars must surely have influenced Lefebvre's team in some way, when they were working on the 2CV project some years later. Lefebvre was thought to be the natural successor to Voisin, whom he admired greatly. He left when the company was liquidated in 1931 and spent a short time at Renault before joining André Citroën, to whom Voisin had introduced him.

At the opposite end of the experience scale, a young Italian named Flaminio Bertoni was commissioned to handle the body styling. Bertoni was a sculptor – he had no previous experience of car design, and therefore, no preconceived notions to hamper him. The PV project bore fruit in April 1934 with the launch of the Traction Avant. Before it appeared at the Paris Salon in October of the same year, 20,000 had already been sold. All aspects of the car were highly praised, both by the experts and the public. It was comfortable, stylish, technically superb; it put other mass-produced cars in the shade.

Meanwhile, at Clermont-Ferrand, one Pierre Boulanger was engaged in the task of designing low-cost housing for the workers at the Michelin factory there. Born in northern France, Boulanger moved to the USA after completing his National Service in the Observer Corps at Sartory, where he flew planes and balloons. He worked as, among other things, a ranch-hand and a tram driver before securing a job as a draughtsman with a firm of architects in Seattle. He moved on to establish his own design and building company in Canada. When war broke out in Europe in 1914, Boulanger returned to France to fight for his native country, rising to the rank of captain in the Armée de l'Air. It was during the war that Boulanger met the Michelin brothers; when the war ended they invited him to join their company designing functional housing for their workers – a practical and demanding task for which his past experience and temperament must have suited him well. Boulanger was an extraordinary man. A man of action, he also possessed great breadth of vision. He was a chain-smoker, and an avid taker of notes. He was clearly not a man to suffer fools, gladly or otherwise.

Unfortunately, the Traction Avant had drained the financial resources of André Citroën's company. Huge amounts of money had been poured into the development of the car, including rebuilding and refitting the factory ready for production to start. Citroën was unable to finance the company personally any further, nor could he find money from elsewhere. Just before Christmas in 1934, the Société André Citroën was officially liquidated. (Ironically, the car whose development bankrupted the company was later extremely successful.) André Citroën collapsed under the strain of his debts and died early in 1935. Michelin, as the principal creditor, protected its interests by buying the company. Pierre Michelin and Pierre Boulanger were installed jointly to restore order and profitability to the troubled firm. They wasted no time. By the end of 1935, Boulanger had sounded out Michelin on the subject of a new car – a car for the ordinary farmer and his family – a car which would, eventually, take over from the traditional horse and cart – the 2CV story had begun.

A Duck is Hatched

Boulanger's brief to Maurice Broglie, his chief engineer, was basic but precise, and totally practical. The car, which was codenamed '*Bécassine*' (Snipe) at this point, was to be an umbrella on four wheels. The 'umbrella' had to accommodate two farmers dressed for work, along with either 50kg of potatoes or a small barrel of wine. The four wheels and their accoutrements should be able to convey the whole in comfort at a maximum speed of 60km/hour and cope with the poorest of roads; and some of the roads were very poor indeed. Economy was a priority; no more than three litres of petrol were to be used to cover 100km, and it must retail at less than one-third of the price of the Traction Avant. A specific 'look' or style was not part of the plan; this car was to be a practical motoring solution to a problem faced by working folk, so looks were unimportant.

Boulanger had spent the previous 16 years of his life in a predominantly rural area of France. He had become convinced that, if the right car could be produced at the right price, it would virtually sell itself. The hard-working farmers would be able to take their produce to market in town quickly and efficiently. To test his theory Boulanger dispatched Jacques Duclos on a five-month-long market-research trip. Potential customers were asked about their motoring needs. What kind of transport do you use? How often do you use it? What do you need to carry? What would you prefer? In all, over 10,000 people from all walks of life were interviewed. It was unusual at that time to find such emphasis being placed on customer research – once again new ground was being broken in the field of marketing by the Citroën concern.

Boulanger must have been convinced of the efficacy of his project, however, because by the time Duclos returned with his data, the project, now known as 'TPV' (*toute petite voiture*) was well underway. André Lefebvre was in charge of a team which comprised Flaminio Bertoni and Jean Muratet, who were responsible for the bodywork; Alphonse Forceau, a gearbox specialist, who also developed the suspension system; Marcel Chinin, who was responsible for co-ordination of bodywork and mechanical components; and Roger Prud'homme, the head of Experimental Design. They produced plans for a chassis-less, front-wheel-drive car weighing less than 300 kilos. A corrugated body, borrowed from the body panels of the Junkers JU-52 plane, would keep weight to a minimum.

Previous pages: Half a century of change: The discreet blue and yellow logo has long gone, replaced by an effective modern corporate image in red and white on the flags. How different would the Citroën story have been without the 2CV? The ancestral 2CV, the 1939 prototype, is quartered at the Citroën head office in Paris, cared for with pride by Marcel Allard.

Below: The early doors had a rounded shape reminiscent of a Bauhaus design; by the time of the launch, the shape of the rear doors had changed, although initially they still hinged on the central pillar. By this time too, door handles had been thoughtfully provided. The cable suspending the seats can be seen through the rear windows.

Right: It is not clear whether this car is the complete surviving model from 1939; some sources believe it survived intact, but more probable is the theory that parts from the cars which were supposed to have been destroyed during the war were crated and kept for posterity. Certainly the car was rediscovered and reconstructed in the early 1970s by Jacques Wolgensinger, Citroën's chief of publicity.

The results of the survey proved Boulanger right. Mechanical transport would be welcomed, but the cars available at the time were clearly unsuitable for the average farmer. They were simply too big and heavy, and unwieldy to handle with ease. Even assuming that the farmer could afford to buy a car in the first place – which was unlikely – the costs involved in keeping one running well were prohibitive. Should such a car be neglected by a hard-pressed owner, it would probably cease to function altogether. The ideal car for farmers would be rugged, comfortable enough (although comfort should not be confused with luxury), cheap to run and maintain, and it would need to keep going with the minimum of attention, even if the owner had little or no mechanical knowledge. Boulanger was also correct in his belief that looks would not be considered a priority – Bertoni's reactions to the customers' perceived value of his contribution are not recorded!

By 1936, a full-size wooden mock-up had been made. Boulanger, who was a tall man, was unhappy with the limited headroom, and ruled that future versions should enable him to drive while wearing his hat. The cornerstone of his philosophy demanded that the car should be designed around people, and fulfil the drivers' requirements. The first prototype appeared at the start of 1937. Aluminium had been used extensively because it was light, and although it was at that time expensive, the team believed that it would soon come down in price. The wheels were made of magnesium, the windows of mica. Cloth, hammock-style seats were suspended from the roof by cables. The engine was not yet ready to be tested, so power was provided by a

500cc BMW motorcycle engine, its kick-start device conveniently replaced with a starting handle. The suspension system comprised several torsion bars, sited under the rear seat. The front-wheel-drive arrangement was a development of that used in the Traction Avant. When this car was tested, it was found to travel at speeds of up to 100km/hour – frighteningly fast in view of the design – and must have reminded Boulanger and Lefebvre of their aviation days.

By the end of 1937, 20 prototypes had been produced. Secrecy had been important to the project – Boulanger was naturally anxious that no other car manufacturer should beat him to the goal. The early cars had been tested at Bois de Meudon, near Paris, but now something a little less public was called for. The grounds of an old château were discovered at La Ferté-Vidame, west of Paris, and a purpose-built, 2.5km track was soon under construction there. Test driving was not a job for the faint-hearted. The early test cars had no roof so the team wore leather flying gear to keep warm.

Although there were still problems, Boulanger must have been pleased with the progress of the project, and happy to have established a secure test ground for it. His responsibilities at Citroën had increased during this year with the untimely death of Pierre Michelin in a road accident. He had also had to cope with a mutiny from within the ranks; a group of the more reactionary designers – no doubt remembering that they had been designing motorised transport for André Citroën when Boulanger was still building houses for Michelin workers – designed a small car of their own. The plot was

Above: The canvas cover survived on the production cars until 1958, although with a larger rear window from the previous year. This system was designed to make the carrying of awkward loads a lot easier.

Above right: Between the wars, there were in excess of 300 independant car manufacturers in France. Lefebvre had worked for Voisin, friend and rival of Bugatti. The curved shape of the prototype 2CV is reminiscent of this 1936 Bugatti T57.

Below right: Not exactly the last word in upholstered comfort, but the famed suspension makes the prototype surprisingly comfortable to ride in.

Left: The 1939 prototype had a single headlamp – all that was required by law at the time. The starting handle was permanently attached. The double chevron shapes can be clearly seen in the engine cover.

Below: The original intention was for the 2CV to have a water-cooled engine. Initial designs were for a single-cylinder unit. The prototype is fitted with a 375cc flat twin engine, designed by Maurice Sainturat, who was also responsible for the Traction Avant engine, from which this car's radiator was borrowed. The engine is maintained in running order.

Right, above & below: The interior of the 1939 prototype. When this car leaves the security of its garage and ventures out into the gardens that surround the Citroën headquarters, it arouses much interest. Visitors to Citroën, and employees, more used to dealing with XMs and AXs, crowd around it, marvel at its idiosyncrasies and its unusual brand of charm.

bought to Boulanger's attention – the 'pretender' vehicle was not heard of again.

The TPV was now fitted with a 375cc flat-twin engine designed for it by Maurice Sainturat. Aluminium was still used extensively for the bodywork, but was causing problems other than those of availability and cost. The work force were totally unused to handling this strange material. It was difficult to weld, and the AEG equipment ordered especially for the job did not arrive in time. Many panels had to be made by hand in the absence of the correct machine tools. Nor were construction problems the only consideration. What satisfied the engineering-oriented test drivers would not necessarily pass muster with the potential customer. The car was too crude. The water-cooled engine and basic suspension were not good enough. A complicated hydraulic anti-dive system, activated by the brake pedal was installed, but it was unreliable. The chassis was too flexible; an aluminium floorpan had been added by Lefebvre to the later prototypes in order to provide support for the body, but the two had to be welded together at various points, and so induced a new set of problems. Furthermore, the chassis had been drilled, in the manner of aircraft production, to save weight, but this had resulted in the chassis flexing. Paradoxically, the light weight of the car meant that, when loaded, the rear of the car would ground, with the nose pointing skywards, in spite of the fact that the proposed solutions to some of the other problems were actually adding to the overall weight of the car.

There were potential maintenance difficulties, too. The oil could not be changed without a pit or ramp; even topping it up was next to impossible. The handbrake worked only intermittently and the petrol filler was easy to break. A tall driver was wrongly positioned for good all-round visibility, and there was no rear-view mirror. Handles were inadequate, and tended to fall off at the slightest provocation. Seats were rough and unyielding, and it was difficult for a tall person to get in and out of the driver's door. The mica windows were easily scratched by the hand-operated wiper and were prone to attracting alarming quantities of dust due to static. Draughts and leaks abounded at every orifice.

Despite all the problems Boulanger still planned to unveil his car to the world at the 1939 Paris Salon. In May he ordered a batch of 250 cars to be built at the factory in Levallois. The Deux Chevaux was clearly not ready to be released and, had the launch gone ahead, it would probably have spelled financial ruin for the Citroën company once again. Only one fully completed example rolled from the production line – at midday on Saturday 2 September 1939. At 11am the following morning, war was declared. The remaining 249 vehicles were in various stages of construction, and some must have been almost finished.

At the beginning of 1934 Ferdinand Porsche presented to the Reich Ministry of Transport his 'proposal concerning the construction of a German people's car.' By 1939 a number of prototypes had been tested, and had passed muster with the authorities, despite initial scepticism. The project was taken under the wing of the KdF (Strength through Joy), the National

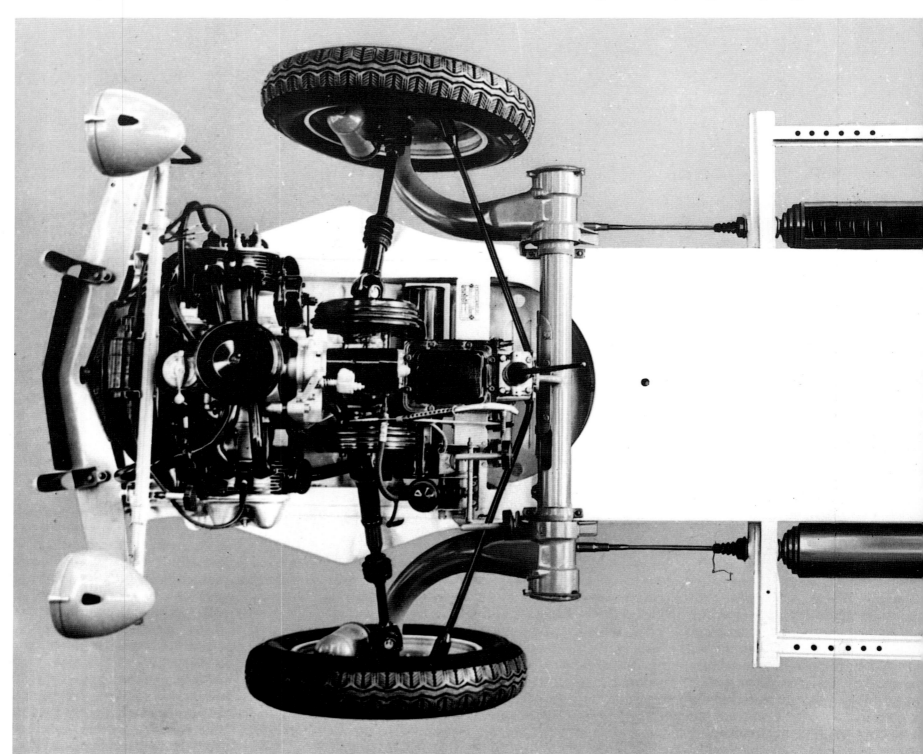

Right: Although designed to facilitate loading, the canvas top could also be used as a sun-roof when people, rather than cargo, were being transported. The rear window section was fixed; 'sunroof' and 'boot' sections could be rolled back independently. Publicity photographs, such as this one from 1949, would have reassured those who found it hard to believe that such a small car could carry four adults in any degree of comfort. The bench seats were basic but comfortable; they were easy to remove and replace – particularly useful for picnics. The covered rear wheel became a distinctive feature of almost every Citroën saloon until the 1980s.

Below: The Citroën 2CV floorpan – simplicity itself.

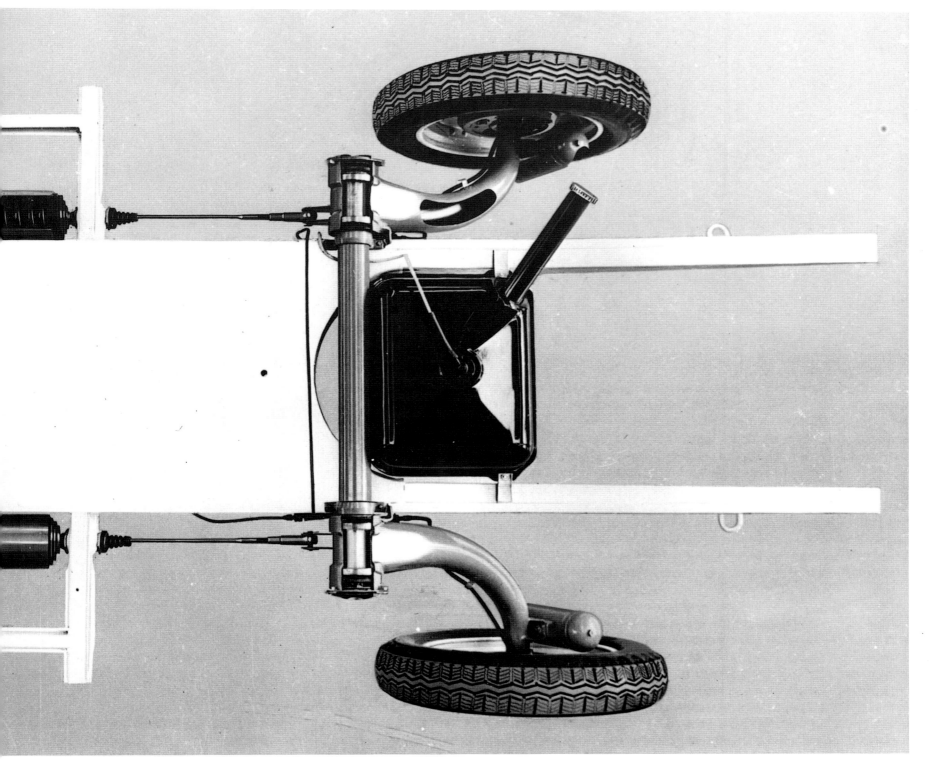

Socialist leisure organisation, and in May 1938, Hitler laid the foundation stone of the new factory. But when war broke out in 1939, the project was put on hold, to be resurrected, like the TPV, when hostilities were over. Whereas the German car was shelved in favour of armament production, however, the Citroën factory was prevented from making cars by the occupying Germans. Boulanger was completely opposed to any form of co-operation with the German authorities. In 1940 they attempted to examine the TPV prototypes, but he refused, even though they offered him their Beetle prototype to look at by way of a swap. So determined was Boulanger that the TPV project should not fall into the hands of the Nazis, that he ordered the remaining prototypes be destroyed.

It was difficult to plan for the future during the Occupation, but despite the gravity of the international situation, there were many who believed that the war would soon be over. Boulanger was of this opinion. He ordered a re-costing of the car – the TPV would, in its present form, now cost 40 percent more than was acceptable. The project returned to the research department, now under the directorship of Jean Cadiou. Despite the strongest inclinations of Boulanger and Lefebvre with their avionic background, the lightweight, but expensive aluminium construction was the first component to go, rejected in favour of steel. Maurice Steck, now in charge of the bodywork, drew up plans for a bodyshell of light-gauge steel.

In 1943 or thereabouts, attempts were made to enhance the appearance of the car; the 1939 version is not a pretty car, and has since been likened to a one-eyed garden shed. However, anyone who has spent time in its company will tell you that it has a definite charm. Bertoni intended to integrate the single headlamp into into the centre front above the grille. He also played with radically different designs, including one in bright yellow, but these did not ultimately find favour with Boulanger.

Walter Becchia, who had arrived at Citroën from Talbot in 1941, having been responsible for the design of the highly successful Talbot-Lago engines, designed a new engine for the TPV, a feat which he accomplished in three days. It was of the same capacity and layout as the original, but air-cooled in an attempt to cure the cold-start problems that had dogged the earlier cars. He also redesigned the gearbox, adding a fourth gear, which Boulanger considered to be an unnecessary complication, as well as defying his specifications. But the Becchia gearbox did find its way into the 2CV, billed as a three-speed box with overdrive. When the first production CVs appeared, they had an 'S' (for *surmultiplé*) on the change-knob. Becchia also created an electric starter at this time, which could be attached to the 2CV's engine. It came into its own just before the Salon in 1948, when the recoil starter fitted to some of the cars was discovered to break fingernails, or worse, the wrists of the unfortunate testdrivers who were often the Citroën secretaries.

Previous pages: The Citroën stand at the 1948 Salon. The bonnets are locked shut – visitors had to content themselves with touching the bonnet, rolling back the hood, and asking questions of the salesman who has been roped off for the purpose with a car to be left untouched – apart from the literature on the bonnet. The salons were always popular. With the war over, people were eager to get on with their lives and make forward progress, but the economic state, both of the country generally and individuals in particular, must have made forward planning very hard. Was this the shape of cars to come? Small, cheap to buy and run, versatile, designed with the ordinary working man and woman in mind – many folk must have left the salon with a new dream forming in their minds. On the next stand is Citroën's previous small car, the Traction Avant. Next door on the Renault stand is the 2CV's rival, the 4CV.

Left: As always, the motoring press would be divided in its opinion of the new car. The daily press covered the Salon, and the new, much-rumoured Citroën got good coverage, lots of it front page material: 'the 2CV Citroën – seats four, five litres to go 100km'. 'Surprise 2 cylinder Citroën steals show'; ' . . . we present the automobile of tomorrow'; 'The 2CV Citroën is the star'; 'Surprise car of the Salon . . . for 185,000 francs'. The words 'surprise' and 'secret' crop up again and again in the reports.

Right: 1952 silver grey 2CV.

The suspension system was also destined for improvement. Boulanger's brief for this change was as disciplined as ever; the car must be able to cross a field carrying a basket of eggs without any being broken. The pilot batch of cars had had compression springs fitted instead of torsion bars, but road-holding was still below par. Léon Renault (no relation to the rival company) had developed a system of spring dampers earlier, but the war had prevented their progress. He returned to Citroën after his war service and reintroduced his largely forgotten original design.

Refinements followed rapidly. After several close shaves, when oncoming motorists mistook the single headlamp for that of a motorcycle and came too close, the testdrivers suggested making life safer by giving it a partner. A simple heating system was added and the hammock seats were replaced with fabric-covered benches. Boulanger's 400-kilo upper-weight limit had now been well and truly exceeded. He had his engineers dismantle and examine every part to find weight-saving options. The team must by now have been starting to lose patience; suggestions included the use of papier mâché and bamboo, hollow bolts and glow-worms instead of lights. Boulanger had to compromise – the car's weight was a *fait accompli*.

Boulanger approved the car for production in February 1948 on the understanding that it would appear at the Paris Salon in the autumn of that same year. Only one colour was on offer – a metallic grey that, to quote the *Architects' Journal* of August 1986, 'matched the exterior walls of Richard Rodgers Lloyds Building.' The practical car was to have a practical name – the 2CV.

And so at the 35th Salon de l'Automobile, on 7 October 1948, after a gestation period of 13 years, the 2CV was officially born. Boulanger unveiled it in the presence of Vincent Auriol, President of the French Republic. Press and public were amazed, intrigued, and bemused. To many of the 1.3 million who viewed the car, most of whom could not previously have considered car-ownership, the potential of the strange, bouncy little beast must have been very exciting.

The bonnet remained sealed at the Salon. Boulanger had no intention of allowing the competition to steal his thunder by rushing a similar, alternative car on to the market; at the previous year's Salon, Lefaucheux of Renault had

unveiled his new 4CV car with the words, 'We shall be unbeatable for years!' Although Citroën were anxious to prove him wrong, 2CV production did not start until 1949. By September of that year the car was at last available in limited numbers and there was soon a waiting list for the Deux Chevaux. Estimates vary, but it is quite probable that a would-be owner would find his attempt to get behind the wheel frustrated for at least a year or two. Boulanger insisted that, as cars became available, priority should be given to those whose work necessitated transport, but for whom ordinary cars were too expensive to maintain and use. Citroën inspectors visited every prospective buyer to check that they fulfilled the criteria; priority went to country doctors, midwives and vets. Many a country farmer must have been relieved to hear the approach of the distinctive, air-cooled sound of the inspector's car which was to become so familiar. The little car was beginning to make its mark.

When the 2CV was first introduced in 1948, there were many who were enraptured. Others could afford to be more high-handed. Indeed, Citroën's own sales personnel had to be forcibly persuaded to sit in the car – although, of course, they became much more positive later, when it started to sell well. Press reaction was mixed. The French newspaper *La Presse* had tried to get itself a scoop by taking a clandestine picture over the walls at la Ferté just before the Salon, but they only managed to snap an old prototype being driven around the track.

Light Car, reviewing the event, called the 2CV the 'Sensation of the 35th Motor Show . . . the most determined attempt so far by a French manufacturer to provide really economical motoring for four passengers.' Citroën, they said, obviously intended to corner this particular market. They summed up: 'Is this what the French people want? Thousands pressed on to the stand all day long, so it must be.' Another journalist however, described the car as 'a grave error'; yet another compared it to a tin can, asking if an opener was provided. *Autocar* said 'The designer has kissed the lash of austerity with a masochistic fervour,' although when they tested it, they praised it highly, calling it well-mannered on the road, and enthusing over its superb engine. Prophetically, the Swiss *Revue Automobile* called the car 'a world beater'.

In 1949, *The Motor* summed up the car thus: 'Among the most interesting

post-war projects from France is the 2CV . . . it is a car which is not merely planned to be exceptionally inexpensive to manufacture and economical of fuel; it is also intended to have that rugged simplicity of mechanical and electrical detail which will allow it to withstand extremes of abuse and neglect in any part of the world.' One year later, The Motor journalists had been able to confirm their positive first impressions by travelling to France for a trial run: 'No one could travel 100 yards in this car without being amazed at the comfort. Despite its small size, the Citroën rides over bumps and pot-holes like the best large American cars. This is no exaggeration. It can be driven up and down kerbs at 20mph without shock reaching the passengers. Even bomb-pocked pavé does not affect the smooth riding. . . .' After a description of the unorthodox suspension, in which the wheel members are likened to the outstretched legs of an animal, the magazine prepares the British reader for the downside. 'Outwardly, this model is almost defiantly crude . . . interior appointments too are functional and stark by British standards, particularly the windows, which are mere flaps hinged at the top.' In peculiarly British style, they pointed out that the hinged windows 'permit speech with the outside world without opening the door.'

When it became available in 1949 the price of the car was 228,000 francs, 43,000 francs more than that quoted a year earlier. Here is the specification of the 1949 car.

Technical Specification of the 1949 2CV

Engine: Flat-twin, air-cooled. *Bore:* 62 mm. *Stroke:* 62 mm. *Capacity:* 375 cc. *Fiscal rating:* 2 CV. *Compression ratio:* 6.2:1. *Max power, bhp (SAE):* 9 at 3,500 rpm. *Max torque:* 14.5 lb-ft at 2,000 rpm. Solex 22 ZACI carburettor with 16.5 mm choke. Ignition contact-breaker mounted on end of crankshaft. 1 mm copper spacer between crankcase and cylinder. Domed pistons. 8-bladed fan. Valve-type oil feed.
Transmission: Single dry-disc clutch; gearbox with four forward speeds, all-synchromesh, plus reverse. Drive shafts with simple universal joints at both ends.
Wheels: 3-inch rims, 3-stud fixing. Michelin 'Pilote' tyres, 125 × 400, tubed.
Suspension: all-independent, linked front to rear. Each suspension arm linked by lever to pull on a coil spring within a cylinder longitudinally installed beneath the chassis. One inertia-type damper per wheel, damping by one rubbing pad per wheel.
Brakes: Drum type, on all four wheels. Front drums 200 mm diameter, rear drums 180 mm. Parking brake on front wheels.
Steering: Rack and pinion, the rack installed within the front axle tube. *Steering ratio:* 14:1. *Turning circle* 10.5 metres.
Electrical system: *Battery* 6 V, 50 Ah; 6 V generator mounted on the end of the crankshaft.
Dimensions: *Wheelbase* 2.40 m; *Front track* 1.26 m; *Rear track* 1.26 m. *Overall length* 3.78 m; *Width* 1.48 m; *Height* 1.60m.
Capacities and weights: *Fuel tank*, 20 litres; *Engine oil*, 2 litres; *Gearbox oil*, 1 litre; *Brake fluid*, 0.5 litre. *Kerb weight* with 5 litres fuel, 495 kg; Fully laden, 800 kg.
Performance: *Maximum speed*, 65 km/hour. *Fuel consumption*, from 4 to 5 litres/100 km.
Bodywork: Bonnet with welded sides and two attachment points. No indicators. One rear lamp. One stop-lamp. Bonnet secured by sliding pin. Badge set in oval front grille. Door latches without locks.
Interior trim: Window operation by spaced rectangular grips. Black steering wheel. No ignition key: starter button on facia. Grey, seamless upholstery.
Colour: Metallic grey. Wheels natural aluminium.

But those first owners were not buying just an unusual set of mechanical specifications. They were the first to own a 'character car' that would become part of the very fabric of French life, and whose appeal would spread far and wide.

Left: A line-up of 2CVs ready to leave the factory, probably in 1953.

Above: There's only one thing it could possibly be. . .

Right: The 1949 Salon. The bonnets are open now, with the engine on view for all to see. The price has risen to 228,000 francs. Although, once the car was popular, it was only just becoming available to the general public, and only then after they had proved their suitability. In 1949, only 924 cars were made, although this figure rose to over 6000 the following year. During the first five years of production, 78,000 2CVs were built. The year of peak production was in 1966, with nearly 170,000 2CVs rolling off the production lines.

On the Road

In 1953, the A model, as the first production 2CV was designated, gained an ignition key and door locks, and now came in a darker grey, with yellow wheels. The bonnet was now made from a single piece of pressed steel, so the welds at the sides were eliminated.

By 1952 the 2CV was being imported into Switzerland. *Automobile Review* enthused that their test car 'turned out to be a solid, pleasant, very versatile and economical car.' They took their car on to mountain passes, and found that it performed admirably, the gearing coping very well with the sharp gradients. They also pointed out that the suspension gave both driver and passengers an immense feeling of security when negotiating the twisting mountain roads, but that from a car following behind, the 2CV's tilt looked positively alarming. They conclude: 'The manufacturer has been generous in just one area; namely in the richness of original and practical ideas that the 2CV incorporates. It can fulfil its task in its present form for years to come.'

Although the 2CV was not available in Germany until 1958, there was much interest in it quite early in its career. The *Das Auto* journalist was surprised that, despite his height and weight, the car accommodated him comfortably. He was not displeased with its speed and performance; his anxiety about the continuous changing of gears proved to be unfounded as he discovered that 'even driving over kerbstones at 40km/hour did not disturb its republican-French equilibrium.' Sceptical when he set out, he had a lot of respect for the car by the end of a day in its company. However he could not come to terms with its outward appearance: 'The ugly exterior remains,' he complained, 'would it really have cost the manufacturer so much more to have given it a somewhat more appetising form?'

Meanwhile in Britain, the 2CV was known as . . . the 2CV. The very quirkiness that made the car so popular in France was one of the reasons for its lack of success on the other side of the Channel. Crippling import duty did not help. The British car market was dominated by home-produced cars and new 'foreign' cars were not particularly popular. A far higher priority was given to comfort – or perhaps it was perceived comfort – than in France or Holland; and even though considerably more expensive than in its native land, the 2CV had better suspension and seating than anything British of comparable price.

The first right-hand drive 2CVs were manufactured at the Slough factory in 1953. From the beginning concessions were made to British tastes. Semaphore indicator arms were positioned just forward of the front doors.

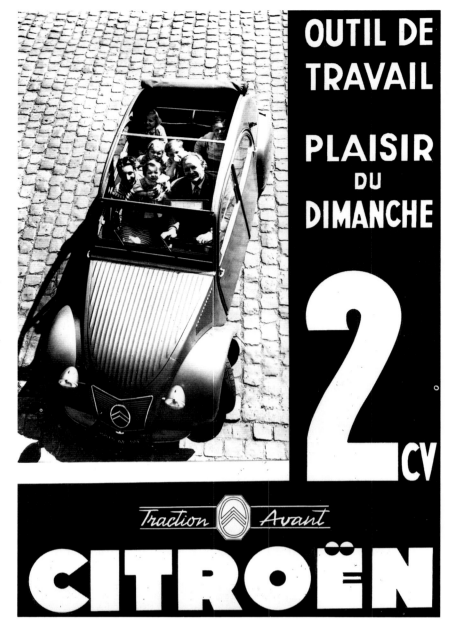

Previous pages: The car on the left is 1957 vintage; although registered in England, it is a French-built car. Oval indicators were added to the rear quarter panels in 1954. The other two cars are from the late fifties.

Above: 'A working tool, and a pleasure on Sunday' – the first Citroën owners obviously put in a six-day week. The 'Traction Avant' logo is still in use for the 2CV in this advertisement from the early fifties.

Left: Another advert from the first five years of its life: 'work, business or pleasure – the 2CV keeps overheads to a minimum.'

Right, above & below: This beautiful silver grey 1953 model belongs to Nick Thompson, who runs 'le TPM' (le Tout Petit Musée) museum of classic 2CVs in Sussex, England.

Pour le tourisme!

Pour les affaires!

Pour le travail!

2 CV CITROËN **pulvérise vos frais généraux**

They were self-cancelling, by means of a pneumatic time switch. The rear windows flapped open in the same way as the standard front ones. Wing mirrors, chromed bumpers and special hub caps helped the transformation; the speedometer was mounted in the centre of the dashboard, illuminated by the interior light (described by *Autocar* as 'similar in shape to an upturned ginger-beer bottle') above the mirror. There were two front seats instead of the single bench seat of the standard French model. The boot lid was metal from the start, enabling the remaining fabric section to be billed as a 'sun-shine roof' in the publicity material. Sitting proud on the centre of the bonnet, the British car's badging was completely unique. A stylised car-front design, about six inches long, sweeps down the centre of the bonnet, its wheel becoming a yellow and blue badge inscribed 'Citroën Front Drive'.

The British motoring press were guarded in their praise for the car. *Motor* ran a car in 1953 for four weeks in all weather and tested it in all types of conditions over 1400 miles. Nine different drivers were involved, of which six came down in favour of the car and two against. (What about number nine? Is it possible to be *neutral* about a 2CV?) *Motor* pondered: 'Whether the 2CV Citroën would meet the needs of, say, the average weekend or business motorist in (Britain) is a debatable question. There can, however, be no doubt of its usefulness where rugged, reliable and economical transport is required, to work within a relatively small radius and with the very minimum of attention.' The conclusion? 'A vehicle with almost every virtue except speed, silence and good looks.' *Autocar* were perhaps saying more than they knew when they wrote, albeit in a slightly perplexed tone: 'There seems to be a definitive 2CV cult in the course of creation, and an extraordinary spirit of camaraderie exists between owners. They wave to each other on the road and eagerly exchange experiences when they meet.'

Motor Sport magazine were obviously 2CV fans of the first order. 'To the obvious question – is the 2CV tedious to drive? – I can answer an emphatic ''no!'' . . . it rides over the worst surfaces better than a Rolls-Royce.' They dismiss the criticism of the car as being too expensive by pointing out that, even allowing for import tax, the price difference over a Morris Minor or an Austin A30 would be recovered after 2000 or 30,000 miles respectively due to the saving in fuel costs. As to the charge that the car is too ugly? 'When you are snug inside the 2CV you cannot see how ugly it looks.' They end their resumé: 'British designers and manufacturers, please copy, if you can!'

Above & left: Nick Thompson's silver grey 1953 car, a French built example in original condition with less than 40,000km on the clock. Compare a side view of this car with one from thirty years later, and you realise just how little the basics of the 2CV have changed.

Above right: The end of the fifties, and family holiday motoring and touring was becoming more popular. The austerity that had followed the war years was over, a new generation of families was growing up.

Right: The 375cc engine of the 1953 car featured left.

Above: A well-used and weathered 2CV parked over lunchtime just around the corner from the café.

Left: 1955, and the Traction Avant is still very popular. It is seen here next to the 2CV and other Citroën stablemates. When the 2CV was first conceived, part of the design brief stated that it must cost only one third of the price to buy, and one third of the cost to maintain, the Traction Avant.

Right: Dunlop, Kleber, Uniroyal – but no Michelin. The original 2CVs ran on Michelin 'Polite' tyres.

DUNLOP

Pneus
Kléber-Colombes

EN VENTE ICI

UNIROYAL

Left: Nick Thompson's 1955 Slough-built car with a 425cc engine, one of only six or so British-built cars known to survive. Bibendum stands guard – his company is an integral part of the Citroën story.

Above left: British built cars were provided with a Semaphore indicator arm, which was self-cancelling by means of a pneumatic switch.

Above right: Only British-built cars had this special front badging. The Traction Avant shape is still there and 'Front Drive' confirmed its pedigree to the British buyer.

Right: The British cars were always fitted with a bootlid, even though their French counterparts still sported canvas. They were not the same as the later French lids, as they sat slightly proud of the surrounding panels, and had no ribbing. The rear badge, again only fitted to British cars, was borrowed directly from the Traction Avant, which was being built at the Slough factory at the time.

Left: The 2CV was designed to carry anything – from the daily bread to the kitchen sink.

Below left: A publicity photograph for the 2CV from the late 1950s.

Right & below: A car from 1958. There were not yet any colour options; the wheels were slightly lighter grey.

In 1955 in France, the AZ model was introduced with a more powerful 425cc engine and centrifugal clutch. Some entirely necessary equipment was added: flashing indicators, window catches, rear and side lights, and a better speedometer. The oval surround to the chevrons on the grille disappeared. Seats were now of tartan-effect material, but there was no choice of colour until 1957, when the AZL model (L for 'luxe') offered a choice of seat and hood colour options. The wheels, steering wheel, bumpers and seat frames were a lighter shade of grey, which all helped to relieve the dullness, and the rear window was larger on this model. The AZLP version (P for 'porte de malle', or bootlid) followed later the same year; it was slightly more expensive and had a demister fitted as standard. As its designation suggests, a

metal bootlid replaced the fabric at the back. Two years later, paintwork colour options were introduced, as was the possibility of a fitted radio. Times were not now as hard for the average French family as they had been. The austerity of the postwar decade was over. Citroën were aware that a market existed for a less spartan car, and these changes kept pace with the gradually increasing need, while not compromising the car's practicality.

By the end of its first decade of production, the Deux Chevaux could be bought in a choice of four models, with a selection of four bodywork colours on the more expensive ones. The car's popularity was growing; it had become known affectionately as the 'Duck' in Holland, a name by which it is known to this day. Obviously, the car had found friends and enthusiasts in

Britain, but for the majority the car was still too unrefined, and represented far too much of a challenge. The 2CV spoke to the intellect, but it also addressed the emotions, for it was impossible to remain neutral about it. Unfortunately, the British did not seem to respond to the car's appeal, and Slough production ceased in 1959.

If the 2CV found limited popularity in Britain, its impact in the USA was even less impressive. The American motoring press were enthusiastic; their nickname for it, 'Flivver', implying cheapness rather than worthlessness. *Motor World* gave the car advance notices such as 'the most sensational car in Europe' and 'France's Model T'. However, when *Road and Track* drove their new test car around town in 1955 they were assailed with cries of 'Homemade job?' and 'Mobile Orange Crate'. *Motor Trend* pointed out that, to put up with the 2CV's idiosyncrasies, you had to be a person who enjoys life, and you must also be the type who can laugh at the leers and jeers of your fellow motorists. Not exactly the same ownership criteria that Boulanger had in mind!

These pages: A 1957 2CV built in France, and now preserved in Britain. The same model was used by two Frenchmen, Jean-Claude Baudot and Jacques Seguela, to circumnavigate the world in 1958-9. Their car, which undoubtedly had a tougher life than the vehicle pictured here, travelled 100,000 km in 400 days. Special modifications included the removal of the rear seats and replacement with a hermetically sealed cupboard, an articulated passenger seat so that it could be used as a couch, and the addition of a shallow strong box to hide valuables.

Above: A late 1960s car surveys Paris.

Left: Those flap-open windows were the cause of much merriment to those who found the 2CV's lack of sophistication a problem. Some members of the motoring press had been bemused or horrified by them.

Right: A 1959 car which has been in general use for much of its life. How many other types of car of thirty years old or more can be seen about their daily work in this sort of condition? Indeed, how many other types of that age are seen at all?

During the first year that the 2CV was imported into the States, only 385 were sold, despite some good reviews. For instance, *Foreign Cars Illustrated*'s eloquent test report ended by stating that the 2CV is practical and a lot of fun, and that very few of the 10,000 Americans who might buy one that year would be disappointed.

For a final comment, we return to *Autocar*: 'Each decade in motoring history has produced one or two cars which have left a deeper impression than their contemporaries, by virtue of special qualities or abilities or an exceptional combination of these.' After describing the Model T Ford and the Trojan with regard to the twenties, the magazine continued: 'Such attributes exerted so strong a pull on human afffections that the cars concerned were practically accepted as animate members of the households dependent on them – ''one of the family'' rather than ''the thing in the garage''. . . . In more recent times it has fallen to France to beget the true successor of those earlier mechanical beasts of burden – the Citroën 2CV.'

A Car for All Seasons

The 2CV underwent its first major facelift in 1960 with the introduction of a new front grille. The heavily-ribbed bonnet was replaced by a smoother affair with only five ribbing lines. The side louvres disappeared in favour of a streamlined air intake. All the locks and catches were improved. The 375cc engine was at last discontinued in 1961. 1962 bought electric windscreen wipers and a proper fuel gauge to replace the filler dipstick that had served thus far. The AZLP was replaced by the AZA in 1963; although the cars looked the same from the outside, the AZAM (AM for AMélioré, or improved) arrived with its improved interior specification and chromed trim, headlamp rims and wiper arms. This was the car that was still in place in 1970, with only two real styling changes in the interim: the addition, in 1965, of a third side window at the rear, and a minor change on the grille, when the chevrons were moved up to the bonnet panel above it.

A new decade brought a change of approach to the car that had now come of age. The old models were superceded totally by two new ones, the 2CV4 with the 435cc engine and 2CV6 with the Ami's 602cc (it was actually a 3CV, but why worry?). The two versions were identical; indicator flashers appeared on the front wings, and the electrical systems were now 12 volt. Seats and interior trim continued to improve.

In 1974 the 2CV was reintroduced to Britain in 2CV6 form only, a right-hand drive version built in France. Its reappearance was welcomed, both by enthusiasts of the old, and a new set of potential customers, who saw it as an answer to the energy crisis. On the other side of the world, in Australia, there was unbounded enthusiasm for the 2CV in some quarters. A *Wheels* journalist said that, were he asked to name the best car in the world, he 'would do so in a single numeral and two letters – 2CV.' The wholesomely honest Citroën, he says, is the mark by which all others should be judged; it is a status-less vehicle. 'It has become accepted as . . . a way of life, an outlook, a philosophy. Its styling, if it can be called that, presupposes nothing. In just over 25 years of mass production, nothing has influenced the basic shape.' Evidently to Francophile Australians, whose numbers go largely unrecorded, the 2CV symbolises France more than 'delicious baguettes, appetising paté, delicious Bordeaux reds, haut coiffure [*sic*] and the Eiffel Tower.'

Previous pages: City cars collect bumps and scrapes as an occupational hazard.

Left, top & centre: 1966 car details – the door handle is less refined than its more modern counterpart, but retains the same basic shape. The indicator in front of the third side window, which was added in 1965, is larger than on the older cars.

Below left: Two cars of the early sixties. 1960 brought the new-style bonnet with five ribs. 1965 saw the addition of small amounts of chrome trim – on wipers, mirror, headlamp surrounds and grille.

Right: The 1966 model with the chevrons on the bonnet. Cars which appear to have no chevrons at all are often from this period; perhaps they fell off, for they can also be seen reattached upside-down on occasion!

Below: A cut-away view of 2CV from 1964-5.

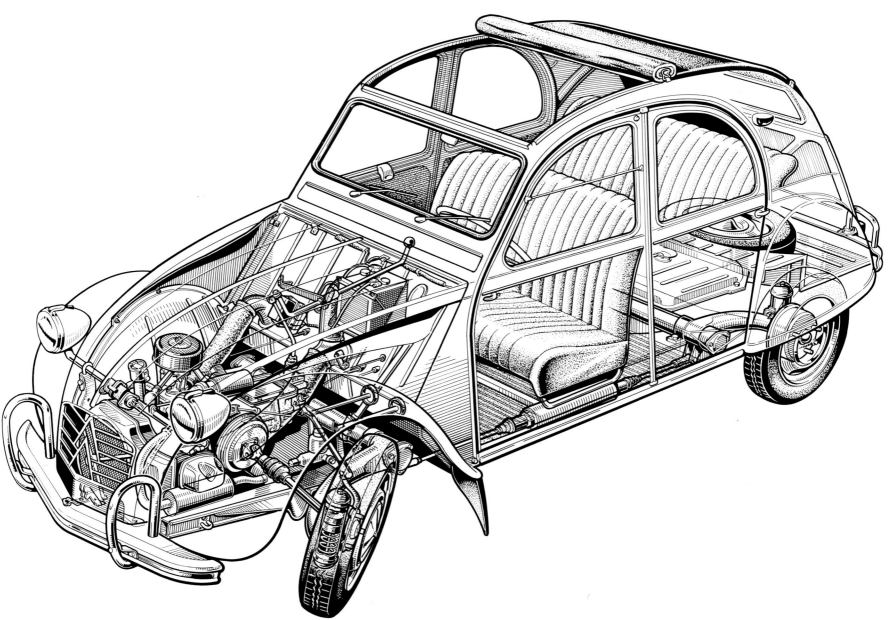

Left & below: No chevrons here – the grille has been replaced – but it still looks like a 2CV! Rectangular headlamps were introduced in 1974, but they were not the most popular of changes; round ones were reinstated by 1981. Ducks don't have square eyes, after all . . .

Right: Twenty-year-old 2CVs which have spent a working life facing the elements, exposed to sun and rain, can get a little faded and matt. This might detract from the appeal of some cars, but with a 2CV it just adds to the character. Many 2CVs of this age are still owned by the same person, or at least by the same family, who bought them from new. They have survived, as was intended when the 2CV was originally designed, with the minimum of maintenance and attention.

Previous pages: Ducks often sit on the riverbank and just think. . . .

Left: Not quite the sort of work usually envisaged for a 2CV but aeroplanes have always been a part of the 2CV story. Both Boulanger and Lefebvre had been involved in aviation and the 2CV bonnet panels were originally borrowed from an aeroplane.

Below: A bright yellow 2CV6 Spécial from 1979. There will still be plenty of good second-hand examples around when the spectators are old enough to drive!

Below right: A suburban Duck.

As with the British, one of the factors that had turned the Australian public off the 2CV in the early days was the spartan specification, while this very unpretentiousness endeared it to the journalists who test-drove it. 'We were impressed by the car's fundamental honesty and amazing behaviour on the road . . . . This car has more unusual and interesting features than all other small cars combined . . . many people consider the car to be ugly. Personally, we think it has a rugged, hard-working look, basically real, and not phoney like the looks of some cars we have seen.' When they described the early cars, they likened their corrugated bonnets to washboards, but far from being an insult, this seemed to confirm their hard-working, no-nonsense image, at least to those who were biased in the car's favour anyway. When reviewing the Charleston, 11 years on, the *Modern Motor* testdriver commented: 'Quite possibly, the Deux Chevaux got it right 37 years ago, and the rest of the world is still out of step.'

There was another change of grille in 1974. This time a plastic one was introduced which incorporated the chevrons, and sat slightly higher on the bonnet. Headlamps became rectangular for the first time. The following year saw the introduction of the Spécial – a cheaper 2CV with older specification, including round headlamps. Initially the car was only available in bright yellow – Bertoni, one of the original designers, would surely have approved.

In 1976, Citroën's first real special edition was launched. This was the Spot (SPecial Orange Ténéré), which was based on the 2CV4, and was one of the first special editions by any car manufacturer. As the name suggests, the car was liberally sprinkled with things orange, both inside and out. The 2CV4 was discontinued in 1979, leaving just two models – the 2CV6 Spécial and 2CV6 Club, which had better-appointed trim and was more expensive. Both were now fitted with the 602cc engines.

During the early 1960s advertising and publicity material for the 2CV took a new turn. Although the accent was still on practicality and versatility, the theme was put across in a different way; it suggested a car that could be whatever you wanted it to be – a practical dream-car! So for the grandmother, the 2CV measures up favourably to her armchair; she sits in it, knitting, with her cat at her feet. For the holidaying family, it's more than a car, it's a life-style. The intrepid explorer assures us that his 2CV can handle life in the open across eight deserts and five continents. A bemused man with an absurd selection of objects to transport, including an old bicycle and a grandfather clock, tells us that his car is obliging and will take anything anywhere. A feature is made of simplicity. The car is being cleaned, with its doors detached and seats removed. A car (very) full of six adults, a child and a dog proclaims '*La liberté!*'

Above: The Spot was the first 2CV Special Edition. In fact, specials were not at all commonplace in 1976, and Spot was one of the first of any make. Their interiors were bright orange and they were fitted with a striped roof-shade. They are not seen very often now; this English Spot is in the process of restoration to its original standard.

Left: If its a Gremlin, it doesn't look very pleased; perhaps it is not that easy to make a 2CV go wrong – best just take a bite out of the grille!

Above right: Flowers were hand painted (on the rest of the car as well) on this English 2CV.

Right: The Americans as a nation never really took to the 2CV, although the Duck has its following there. They obviously never met this cleverly painted example from England, sporting their national flag.

The Ugly Sisters

When the 2CV ceased production in Slough in 1959 a new car was planned specifically for the British market. Citroën attempted to present a conventional-looking saloon car to the British. It was aimed at the growing second-car market – a shopping car, with a boot, made from glass-fibre, and therefore corrosion-free. That car was the Bijou. Introduced at the Earls Court Motor Show in the autumn, it was styled by Peter Kirwan-Taylor, who was also responsible for the Lotus Elite.

The Citroën DS saloon was popular in the UK at this time, and so Citroën planned that the Bijou should reflect some of its glory. From the rear, there were styling echoes of the DS, but the family resemblance was not very strong, and was not at all apparent from the front. Some of the fittings were actually DS parts, although whether this was a styling exercise or an economic one is debatable. The car was two door; the rear seats had little room, reflecting the traditional image of a second car. Fuel consumption was good and the car was not uncomfortable. Tall drivers, however, found their visibility restricted by the top of the windscreen. The Bijou was available in five different colours and the chrome-look bumpers were a styling concession – being attached to the body, they were little more than trim.

This car was no more successful than the right-hand drive 2CV had been. It was more expensive than the competition – the Morris Minor and the Mini for example – and both these cars had the advantages of being British. Bijou production ended in 1964, with less than 250 having been made. Only 50 examples survive to this day.

Until 1955, Citroën's 'other car', the Traction Avant, had been a pres-

Previous pages: A charming Dutch Ami 8.

Above: The attempt to echo the shape of the DS in the Bijou was not successful. Only at the rear is there any slight resemblance, and even then it takes imagination.

Left: The driving position inside a Bijou is most peculiar. Unless the driver is uncommonly short, eye-level is right at the top of the windscreen; when going downhill, visibility is thus reduced to about 10 metres!

Above right: The real things – a DS and a 2CV.

Right: The front of the Bijou shows a certain charm, but not enough to appeal to the English small car buyer. Fewer than 250 were ever made.

tigious model. It was advanced for its time, but was now looking decidedly dated, and the more up-market sector, unlike 2CV territory, was an area where style counted. Some of the same team which brought the 2CV into being had been busy with the Traction's successor, the DS. Advanced in some areas, even today, in 1955 it was sensational. For the next five years, until 1960, the extremely complex DS range ran alongside Citroën's mechanically simpler 2CV. By the end of the 1950s, people had more money in their pockets and a higher standard of living generally. Citroën deemed it the right time to fill the gap in the model range and compete with the new

models from Renault and Peugeot at the same time. Development costs would be kept to a minimum by using all the background knowledge and mechanical know-how of the 2CV. The new car, the Ami 6, was introduced at the Paris Salon in 1961. It comprised the chassis, suspension and steering of its forerunner, but was fitted with a 602cc version of the engine. It was capable of 100km/hour (62 mph) and was economical to drive.

As with the Bijou in Britain, there was an attempt to strike a family resemblance with the DS, especially with regard to interior trim and finishing. But with its reverse-angled rear window and rather alarming demeanour – it had neither the low sleekness of the DS or the cheeky charm of the 2CV – the Ami could not be described as a pretty car. Nevertheless, it was very comfortable indeed, and rapidly found favour with the French car-buying public. In the late 1960s the Ami was France's top-selling car. It was also popular in Germany, where, it was claimed, 'The Ami 6 is what the 2CV can never be.' A reviewer from *Mot* begged his readers not to be deceived by outward appearances. A close look would reveal some very well-planned details. He was also taken with the interior, particularly the cosmetic touches; gold-effect knobs, imitation leather coverings, everything well-applied, smart, and practical. 'The Ami 6 is built with utmost simplicity. Simple parts are simply assembled. What is important (powerplant and chassis) is good and very accurate; everything else is regarded as not so important.'

An estate version was produced in 1964, with a tailgate that allowed a full-depth loading into the quite spacious interior. Both mechanically and with regard to trim, the Estates were identical to Saloons of the same vintage. Both were available in two versions – the standard Tourisme and the more expensive Confort. As well as four- and five-seater versions, the Estate range boasted a Commerciale (later called Enterprise) with Tourisme trim, folding rear seat and flat floor.

In 1968 the engine was uprated and Club versions of both Saloon and Estate were introduced; their most instantly recognisable feature being the twin headlamps. A year later, the Ami 6 made way for the Ami 8, which was launched at the Geneva Motor Show. Estate and Enterprise versions became available later that same year, their relative specifications echoing those of

Above left: The reverse-raked rear window and pointed rear roofline, combined with the 'frown' at the front, contrive to give the Ami 6 a rather stern expression at first sight. Citroën billed it as the most comfortable medium sized car in the world – to which it certainly had a claim. This is a Club version, which had a pair of headlights on each side.

Below left: The non-Club saloon version, and the Estate, like this one, had a single headlight at each side. Ami Estate versions appear to have a plethora of side windows – especially when they are open – as they slide back and forth.

Above: Ami interiors – this is a 6 saloon – are generally well appointed. There was, once again, an attempt to recreate the feel of the DS, which is more successful with the Ami, and particularly noticeable with the interiors.

Right: The styling of the sides of the Ami 8 is similar to the 6. The Ami Club's lines were accentuated with full-length chrome trim.

Left: The interior of the Ami 8. Ami seats are very comfortable indeed. This white car from Holland with its bright red seating and smart, well-preserved instruments is an excellent example. In the sixties, the Ami was France's top-selling car – unlike the Bijou in England, it complemented the 2CV with a character all its own. Popular in both France and Holland, they are less often found in England, although even here there is a club for Ami enthusiasts.

Below: The rear of the Ami 8 was completely redesigned. From the rear, it does have that sweeping line of the DS, accentuated by the covered wheels.

Right: The front of the Ami 8 was simpler than that of the 6; the rather confusing selection of grille lines, angles and curves was streamlined.

their '6' predecessors. The bodywork of the Ami 8 represented a complete facelift of the '6', although mechanically and in terms of equipment they were largely the same. Interior trim, door handles and finishing details were improved. Handling was improved by the addition of an anti-roll bar. There were two versions, the basic Club, and the Confort. In 1970 a new range, the GS, was introduced. Featuring an air-cooled flat-four, the car had pneumatic suspension like the DS. Its 1000cc engine is important here because, in 1973, it was shoe-horned into the Ami Super, the most powerful of the Amis, produced in Saloon, Estate and Enterprise versions. It was closely related to the '8' and was produced until 1975, the Ami 8 surviving until 1979.

Citroën had not originally intended the 2CV in its more basic form to continue thus far. At the Paris Salon in 1967 they introduced a replacement that fitted between the 2CV and the Ami 6 – the Dyane. It was built on the 2CV chassis, with the 425cc engine, but many of the mechanical parts, including the brakes, were of Ami descent. Dyane was clearly of the same family. Its basic body shape looked very similar to its elder brother, but was in fact quite new. The front end was less anachronistic, the lines sharper. The square headlamps were more conventionally placed on the wings. There was a much greater glass area, and the rear end comprised a hatchback/sunroof combination; the roof could be opened from inside the car. There was a choice between two levels of trim: Luxe, and Confort, which provided a slightly higher specification and more load room, having the spare wheel positioned under the bonnet.

In 1968 the engine was replaced with the 435cc unit to give the Dyane 4, while a version with the 602cc Ami engine was introduced as the Dyane 6. Moulded armrests were among the added interior refinements that came with the Dyane 6. A centrifugal clutch was an option for both cars, as was vinyl trim and a folding rear seat, which gave added load space. Like the 2CV five years previously, the Dyane got a third side window in 1969. The Dyane 6 was fitted with the Ami 8 gearbox from this date. The Dyane 4 was discontinued in 1974, and the Dyane 6 became a two-model range with the introduction of the 'week-end' version, which included separate front seats, folding rear seats and a removable luggage platform. Until 1977 changes were confined to a new grey plastic grille, stainless steel bumpers, a push-button boot catch and hazard warning lights. Front disc brakes now became standard equipment, and the grille and handles changed to black.

There were special editions of the Dyane, too. The Caban, which was dark blue with white coachwork, and the yellow-and-black Capra, were only available in southern Europe. The last special edition was the Côte d'Azur, slightly reminiscent of the France 3 version of the 2CV. Dyane production was phased out in 1982, but the 2CV kept on going. Whereas the 2CV was seen as ugly, but highly original, the Dyane was regarded by many as merely ugly. Even so, the Dyane has a following of its own, and there are those who talk about their cars with the same fondness as owners of more conventional Ducks do. However, to quote *Road and Track*, 'Like the Ami before it, the Dyane could not outlast the car it was meant to improve upon. This was because the Ami and and Dyane were unconscionably ugly, while the 2CV was consciably ugly, or beautiful.'

Above: The Dyane was the first hatchback proper produced by Citroën.

Left: The interior and dashboard of the Dyane had a more 'hi-tech' feel than those of the 2CV. It was intended that the Dyane fit into the range between the 2CV and the Ami; a niche which it filled from 1968, when production started, until the end of the Ami's production lifetime.

Above right: The Dyane was billed as offering a sophisticated alternative to the more rustic charms of the 2CV. It has a slightly more modern demeanour; the headlights, incorporated into the wings, and streamlined grille in particular have this effect, although the family resemblance to the 2CV is still very strong.

Right: This working Dyane from Holland belongs to the owner of a garage specialising in Citroën, and is fitted with a GS engine. Although Dyane enthusiasts are usually fans of the duck family generally, the Dyane has a strong following of its own.

What do a Spanish policeman, a Swiss doctor and a North African petroleum engineer have in common? In 1957 Jacques Duclos took to the road again. This time he was checking up on information that had filtered back to Citroën from a number of their dealers – that there was a market for a four-wheel-drive car in the 2CV mould. Low cost and the ability to run on and on without too much attention would be obvious advantages of such a vehicle. Air-cooling meant that neither frozen wastes nor scorching deserts would affect its performance. Air, as the advertising literature pointed out, is always available in unlimited quantities.

Four prototypes were built, and the Sahara, as it was known, was launched to the press in 1958 at Mer de Sable in the Forêt de Compiègne, a military testing ground 50km from Paris. A journalist who test drove it commented, 'This vehicle is intended for the Sahara, for example, and has already gained a nickname; the mechanical donkey! When driving down the same slopes that one has just climbed, one does not have the unpleasant sensation of falling into an abyss, as is the case with previously known vehicles – built with bone-hard springs for military purposes. This is because the passengers are not exposed to hard jolts and the changes of speed in various directions are somewhat subdued.'

Two years later, the Sahara became commercially available. It had two 425cc engines, one placed conventionally, the other in the boot area. The boot cover was replaced by a panel with integral air intakes. The clutch was

hydraulic and there were two gearboxes, operated by a single lever, although the rear unit could be disconnected, and the car driven in two-wheel-drive form, which was particularly useful in road traffic. If the front engine failed, the rear could be used alone too. The rear engine usurped the spare wheel, which was rehoused on top of the bonnet, which had a specially designed recess. Two petrol tanks sat under the front seats, their filler pipe caps sitting in each of the front doors. The suspension was set slightly higher than normal, to facilitate travel over rough ground. There were extra air-intakes above the rear wings, which were cut away slightly. The interior was standard 2CV, although an indicator was added to show the driver the angle of the front wheels. Tyres were wider and bumpers sturdier.

In 1961 a Sahara was driven over high sand dunes in France to put its abilities to the test. It took the climb in its stride, enough evidence of its abilities for the Spanish police to purchase 80 Saharas. They were particularly popular in Switzerland, especially with doctors, and in the desert areas of North Africa; the Sahara's working lifestyle was a tough one. Less than 700 were made and few of the cars survive today.

A rather different utility vehicle was produced in 1968. It was aimed at both ends of the spectrum as far as customers were concerned – the military and the sun-seeker. Versatility was the name of the game with the Mehari; it was also expected to be used as a general workhorse and load carrier.

The Mehari was built on the standard Dyane chassis with strengthened

Left: The Sahara's spare wheel sits on the specially recessed bonnet, leaving space in the rear for the second engine. This is a Swiss example.

Right: The ultimate working 2CV? Vents for the rear engine can be seen on the rear quarter panel. The wings are cut away above the rear wheels.

Below: Another of the 2CV family carrying its spare on the bonnet – a four-wheel-drive Mehari. In this case, the wheel's resighting frees extra space in the rear. The name is derived from a North African camel, famed for its ability to carry heavy loads for long distances.

sections, and was fitted with the 602cc engine. The body has an open cab, with optional roof. Even the doors can be removed. The fabric covering the top is in two parts, front and rear. The press launch was in Deauville, on the north French coast. It has been unkindly described as an overgrown motorised golf caddy, and indeed, one of Citroën's advertising brochures showed it being used for just such a purpose. It had a rugged persona, and was named after a species of North African camel that is appreciated for its toughness. It was made from soft plastic which re-formed easily when subjected to minor bumpings and dentings and was also very easy to clean, inside and out.

The first Meharis had only two seats, but they were soon made with four. Mechanical alterations have generally taken place alongside those of the Dyane. 1979 brought the four-wheel-drive version, with its distinctive headlamp grilles, although these were later fitted to both versions. As with the Sahara, the spare wheel sat on top of the bonnet. It was possible to switch to two-wheel drive if required, and also to lock the differential.

Citroën soon recognised the potential of Mehari in more remote parts of the world. Variations abounded; the Baby Brousse was built in Iran and the Ivory Coast in the late 1960s and early 1970s; the Dalat in Vietnam. Both these versions had metal body panels. The FAF, (*facile à fabriquer, facile à financer*), produced in Senegal, Guinea and the Ivory Coast in 1978, was made of welded metal panels. The vehicle has also been used as the basis for a kit – the Emmit being one of the more popular.

Citroën's advertising literature for Mehari concentrated on its versatility and ability to cope with all conditions. One brochure, mechanical specification apart, is almost entirely composed of photographs; Mehari on the sand, wheel-arch deep in snow, towing a boat trailer, climbing a steep muddy hill. There was a special edition, the Mehari Azur, which appeared in 1986. It has a more substantial top, the seats are wide-striped and the bodywork is white. This version was most definitely aimed at the sun-seeker rather than the adventurer.

Left: The Mehari is made of tough plastic panels, so although they can appear weather-beaten, Meharis today tend to look well-used rather than decaying, as they would if they rusted.

Below left: The Mehari four-wheel-drive dashboard is made of the same tough moulded plastic, which gives it a practical, no-nonsense feel. The black knob is the gear-change. With the white one it is possible to switch between four-wheel and normal drive. The red knob controls the lockable differential.

Right: The Mehari engine is the standard 602cc unit with altered gearbox ratios.

Below: Meharis have always found popularity in areas of rural France where the going can get tough, especially in less than perfect conditions.

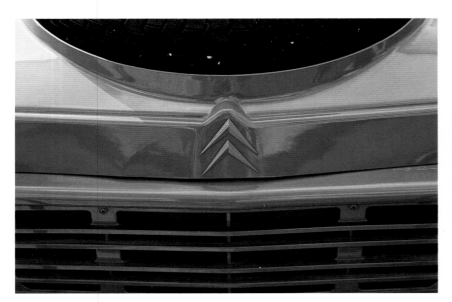

Above far left: The famous Citroën chevrons on the Mehari bonnet.

Above left: Sometimes called the Dyane-Mehari 6, the original Mehari version was not four wheel drive, but instrumentation was very similar on both versions. Dashboards were simply self-coloured panels in the same finish as the exterior, with the minimum of fuss and refinement.

Left: In the early sixties, there had been a series of advertising photographs taken showing the 2CV loaded to the roof and beyond with a variety of objects, including a grandfather clock, cello and bicycle. This is recreated for a motor show stand.

Above & right: Ideal as a working vehicle, the Mehari's top could be completely removed. As the interior was plastic, it could be hosed down with ease, with no worries at all about rust. The huge load space made the Mehari a very attractive proposition.

Commercial Variants

The Mehari served to emphasise how startlingly good the 2CV concept was. It was not the first 'load carrier' of the Duck family. The original fabric top had been designed for ease of shifting large objects rather than for appreciating the sunshine, and commercial van versions – known as the 'fourgonette' in France – had been produced almost from the start. 1951 saw the appearance of the AU van, which was fitted with the 375cc engine and had a payload of 250kg. The 425cc engine was installed in 1954, and the van became the AZU. In 1963 the AK van was introduced with the Ami 602cc engine and a payload of 350kg; the payload was increased to 400kg in 1970, and it became the AKS. A special-edition AZU was produced in 1972 with the 435cc engine, and called 'Grandes Administrations'.

In 1961 a series of carefully crafted photographic statements were united to form a brochure on the AZU. Each image showed someone with the large, difficult, fragile or oddly shaped cargo that they needed to carry around in the course of their business. The characters included a florist, greengrocer, salesman and a deliverer of hats. The van, naturally enough, could cope with them all.

Previous pages: A 1957 2CV van.

Left: A weathered 1957 2CV van with distinctive corrugations; it has been in daily use for most of its life. In its earliest advertising material, the 2CV van, sometimes described as a corrugated tin shack, was billed as having been ' . . . specially built for work and pleasure. All the amenities of a car with all the advantages of a delivery truck. Especially built for transporting breakable goods, expensive special packaging is unnecessary, thanks to the soft suspension . . . . an extraordinarily solid and indestructable vehicle.'

Above & right: This beautifully restored 2CV van sells fish outside the Art Deco Michelin building in London. It has no seats, as the space is used for extra storage space. Although theoretically drivable, the van is usually to be found loaded to the roof with crustacea!

There was a 'Week-end' version in the AZ series, with a second row of re-movable seats and a second window in the rear. Citroën's advertising focused on versatility: 'Comfortable – At your command it can become a comfortable four-seater or a roomy delivery van. The rear seat can easily be removed and the passenger seat folded forward. Practical – specially built for work and pleasure, the "Week-end" offers all the comfort of a car and all the practical advantages of a delivery truck. There is enough space for four people and their luggage for touring, camping or hiking; not only in superb comfort and safety, but with a unique panoramic view.'

Sooner or later, most of the changes to the saloons found their way on to the vans. In 1963 the body ribbing was removed from the middle upwards, which made it easier for signwriting, and a window was added to the side panels. The rear windows also became larger. Later models were produced with an extra 25cm of body height – a hinged flap above the door giving access to the whole load space. 1969 brought a new body, with the ribbing now understated in the same way as the bonnet, and 35cm of extra height was added. Both versions were produced without side windows in 1975, but the windows were back two years later by popular demand.

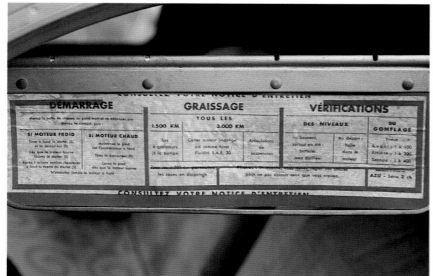

Left: A 2CV van with its saloon counterpart.

Below left: The French Post Office ran fleets of vans for many years. This one has found its way to England.

Above: Mirror detail of the 1957 2CV van. Most of the detail changes of the saloons, both 2CV and Dyane, eventually found their way on to the respective commercials, although sometimes not until a while later.

Above right: The 1957 van. On top of the sun visor is an original list of instructions; how to start the engine when hot and when cold, which items should be serviced and how often, and tyre pressures.

Right: The Acadiane was the commercial version of the Dyane, with which it shared all front panels.

Left: The rear of the Acadiane. The van versions of both 2CV and Dyane are extremely spacious. They have a flat loading area and a surprising amount of width to the doors.

Below: Red Acadiane 'Weekend' version had an extra row of removable seats, which could be taken out to convert the van for daily duties. This version also had an extra side window; some export models had one single large window.

Above right: Big brother to the 2CV and Dyane commercials, the HY van, which shares the family resemblance of corrugations. Another Citroën which sits outside the Michelin building in London; this one sells flowers.

Right: Plain panels were introduced to the vans to facilitate signwriting.

Pick-up versions of the commercials have been available from time to time – the AP (375cc) and AZP (425cc) – were simple variations on the van theme, with a cut-down body. The pick-ups were transportable by helicopter, and were extensively used by the French army. Thirty right-hand drive AZPs were also sold to the British Admiralty in 1958.

Many load-carrying variations were produced in other countries. An estate car was built in both Spain and Iran, and from Chile came the Citronetta, with its strange box-shaped rear end. Over-size bootlids and boxes have long been popular in Holland. An unusual French conversion by ENAC produced in 1962 was the AZC Mixte. The rear opening was hinged above the back window and the back seats folded flat. The floor panel was flat, giving access to a large load area. The spare wheel was relocated under the bonnet. In 1965, two levels of trim were introduced, the AZL and AZAM.

If it is difficult to feel dispassionate about the 2CV, this is doubly true of the commerical versions, very often known as the 'Camionette', or simply as 'Kombi'. Nothing is guaranteed to send a Francophile into raptures as the

ik ben | lid van | citroën-club | "waggel"

unique sight of a working, old-style corrugated version – slightly dented and matt, mud on the rear, chicken feather or stray cabbage leaf adhering somewhere – careering at a seemingly impossible angle along a winding country road. Conversely, nothing is more certain to annoy the person who finds the French way of life not at all to his liking. Hence such epithets as 'dustbin on wheels' and 'corrugated tin shack', the latter also often heard in relation to the 'big brother' of the Citroën Commercial range, the HY.

Both AZU and AKS were discontinued in 1978 and replaced with the Acadiane. This was built on a stretched version of the AK series chassis, and had a payload of 440kg. The front panels were those of the Dyane. Like its precursor, it became extremely popular with small businesses. All the commercial versions lend themselves to conversion. There are caravan conversions galore – everything from the 'second seat removed, sleeping bag in the back' variety, to vans of extended height with bunk beds, cookers, tables – kitchen sinks too. All the 2CV van variations have been in great demand as public service vehicles – particularly as postal vans in rural areas of France.

These pages: This smart Dutch Acadiane has a surprise in store; it is totally fitted out as a camping conversion, with cooking facilities and kitchen sink included. Clever storage facilities in the side save space in the van.

A Different
Kind of Challenge

It was surely inevitable that a car designed from the start to be completely practical and rugged should find its way into adventures of all kinds. Michel Bernier set the ball rolling as early as 1952 by taking a 2CV on a Mediterranean circuit. If that sounds less than arduous, imagine the difference that 40 years has made, both to the number of roads that exist, and to their quality. The following year, he set out again, this time with another Citroën salesman, Jacques Duvey, for Oslo, from where they started the Monte Carlo Rally, although they finished unplaced. Two years later, this determined gentleman was to be found taking part in the Mille Miglia, and finished 271st out of over 600 competitors!

In 1953 Jacques Cornet and Henri Lochon travelled from Canada to Tierra del Fuego in a 2CV – stopping off briefly at Mount Chacaltaya in Bolivia to beat the altitude record for a motor car at 5420 metres! In 1954 *Motor Sport* magazine took a 2CV to Wales; 30 years previously, a six-day-long trial over a difficult course for small cars had been organised by the Royal Automobile Club. The cars had all been standard production models; in addition to negotiating 1924-style Welsh mountain tracks and minor roads, they also took part in time trials on steep gradients, and then went to the Brooklands track for speed and acceleration tests. The tests were very exacting, and included the measuring of fuel and oil consumption and the maintenance of a minimum speed. The magazine decided to see how the 375cc French car performed. While pointing out, fairly, that 30 years had seen at least partial surfacing of some of the roads, they were very impressed by the manner in which the little car overcame obstacles of all types: 'the manner in which the 2CV pulled itself through slime, climbed out of the track on to grassy banks when this seemed expedient, motored unconcernedly through foot-deep water and ploughed through tall bushes was little short of miraculous.' They also pointed out that, when they did get bogged down, the car was light enough to be rescued with minimum fuss and effort. The reviewer concludes, 'This excursion . . . set the seal to my already very favourable opinion of the baby Citroën. It is a fascinating, splendid little car, to which I would gladly give permanent shelter in my garage. . . . Certainly from now on I shall look with scorn on cars of low-power output which employ heavy lumps of cast-iron surrounded by water for engines.'

No prizes for guessing which car was the first to drive around the world; ten years after its launch, Jacques Séguéla and Jean-Claude Baudot set off from the Paris Salon in their 2CV. By the time they returned to Paris the following year, they had completed 100,000 kilometres (62,140 miles). They paused briefly in Chile when the drain plug from the gearbox fell out, and with

it, the oil. They were marooned for a few hours until an enterprising local stuffed the gearbox with bananas. This improvised lubrication not only got them moving, but lasted for 300 kilometres. The Chilean banana merchant has been revered by Citroën mechanics ever since. This car is now in the Le Mans Motor Museum, having been bought by Citroën on its return.

In the late 1960s Citroën decided to offer a prize for the best long-distance journey made in a 2CV each year. The idea proved so popular that they were inundated with requests for sponsorship. Jacques Wolgensinger, who was in charge of Citroën publicity, organised a 'Raid' or rally, an adventure trip for many cars travelling together. Citroën had organised something similar in the 1920s and 1930s to publicise the durability of their vehicles. So in 1969 25 Meharis covered the 15,000km (9,321 miles) from Liège to Dakar and

Previous pages: 2CV Cross always provides plenty of action.

Above: The sport is particularly popular in Holland, with a thriving club full of enthusiasts.

Left: Safety rules are strict; cars are all fitted with rigid roll cages. Steel panels over the roof protect the drivers; side glass is removed in favour of mesh grilles. Harnesses and crash helmets must be worn.

Above right: Enthusiasts travel many miles, towing their Cross cars on trailers behind them, to take part in meetings all over Europe.

Below right: Once the race is underway, its every man and Duck for himself. Some like to get on to two wheels as soon as possible!

Below: As the popularity of 2CV Cross has grown, it has become an attractive proposition for sponsorship.

Left and right: If you start off on two wheels, there comes a point . . . of no . . . return! Although such crashes are spectacular, the safety precautions and relatively low speeds mean that there are rarely serious injuries.

back. The following year, 1970, 500 2CVs and derivatives gathered for the start of a rally from Paris to Kabul and back to Paris, following the 1931 route of Citroën's Croisière Jaune, in which ten Citroën-Kégresse half-track vehicles had taken part. Some 320 returned within the set time limit, having completed 16,500km (9,942 miles) in all. The 1971 rally was for 602cc engine types only, and 500 cars drove from Paris to Persepolis and back again. The participating cars were pelted with stones in Turkey, but given a hero's welcome in Iran; new cars were offered by Citroën as prizes for the best tape recordings and photographic records of the trip.

The last, and the hardest, rally, the 'Raid Afrique', took place in 1973. It was restricted to 602cc cars under five years of age. Hundreds applied to go, and a rigorous selection procedure reduced them to 100 people in 60 cars. The care and forethought was necessary because the high spot of the trip, from the Ivory Coast to Tunis, was to be the conquest of the Ténéré desert, never before crossed by motor vehicle. Trucks led the cars across in groups of 12 but there were no mishaps, all the cars arriving safely in Tunis after a journey of 8000 kilometres (4971 miles).

In addition to these organised events, of course, there were many individual expeditions made in the company of a trusty 2CV. Stories abound of small groups of two or three friends packing their belongings into their Deux Chevaux, and taking off for months at a time. In 1971 two firemen set off from Chile in their Citronetta on a journey that would take them through Central America, across the USA from west to east, around Europe including Scandinavia, and half way across Africa. A tale is told, which may well be true, of two Swiss schoolmistresses who set out on a nine-month trip to retrace the outline of the ancient Roman Empire in a 2CV converted to a camper. Their journey, which centered around the Mediterranean Sea, covered three continents and crossed three deserts. At the end of the journey, the teachers had among their souvenirs a rock collection, a sack of potatoes acquired as a present from some grateful farmers and a 17-year-old German poet.

Left above & below: Competition on the track is fierce, but usually friendly. From the beginnings of the sport, there had been friendly rivalry with a sense of camaraderie – a joy in participating with other lunatics of like mind.

Right: Dirty work was afoot at this Dutch 2CV Cross meeting. Paul Moerman found his car just not its usual self during practice. Lack of power and clouds of white smoke suggested to Paul that the fuel tank had been tampered with. Draining the tank revealed the dastardly presence of evil diesel. Paul reached for his marker pen and spelled out on the car 'Cannot be stopped – even by diesel!' (in Dutch at the back, English at the front). Tank and fuel lines flushed out, Paul was ready to go again, and won against the odds.

A different kind of challenge began to intrigue Duck owners in the early 1970s. Citroën themselves introduced 2CV Cross – originally called Pop-Cross. It aimed to provide an inexpensive form of motorsport in which all could participate, making good use of thousands of 2CVs available. The first meeting was arranged and run by Citroën in a disused quarry at Le Péchereau, near Argenton-sur-Creuse, in July 1972.

The events rapidly became very popular. The following year there were three events in France, two in Portugal and one in Belgium. By 1974 there were seven French events and three in Spain. The first British event was held at Blackbushe in 1975, by which time there were similar events being held in Holland, Switzerland and Austria. The meetings were instigated initially by Citroën themselves, with the organisation being handled by local clubs and enthusiasts. No entry fee was charged, so there was no danger of the sport becoming too commercial. By the end of the decade it had become so popular that clubs had sprung up in every country where second-hand 2CVs were to be found, and organisation of the events passed from Citroën.

Part of the reason that 2CV Cross was so immediately successful was its accessibility. While a great deal of skill is shown – especially by those who have had a lot of practice – no training is necessary and no expensive equipment or technology is required. Although it looks anything but, 2CV Cross is actually very safe; maximum speeds reached are only 70km/hour (43mph).

There are very few injuries that affect anything other than the ego. Strict regulations, both for qualification and safety, are laid down. All cars are required to have a roll-cage and harness, and a reinforced rigid roof above the front seats; side glass is removed, and a metal windscreen grille fitted. The petrol filler cap is fitted with a non-return valve to prevent trouble when the car rolls over, and a maximum of five litres of petrol is carried. Back doors are removed entirely; front doors and bootlid are welded shut.

There are to be no tricks for increasing the power of the engine; mechanical parts must be of the original specification, whether 425/435cc or 602cc. Winning cars may have their engines dismantled on occasion to check that they are completely standard. Some element of modification is permitted, to the exhaust system for example. Some reinforcement of the chassis is allowed, indeed essential. Bars are welded at the front of the engine to prevent bodywork meeting fan in the inevitable collisions. The suspension can be strengthened too, provided only standard Citroën parts are used, and the amount of suspension travel is reduced slightly.

2CV Cross is fun to watch: cars spin, cars roll, cars land on their roofs – and are promptly turned the right way up again and carry on. Bits fall off – and are bolted back on again. Citroën's original concept of a fun sport – safe, but with real excitement, entertaining for everyone, participant and spectator alike – still holds good today.

Above: When is a duck not a duck? These two fine examples of Charon coachwork really are Duck-based. The one on the left is based on a 2CV, with a Traction Avant-style grille incorporated. The one on the right is based on a Dyane.

Left & right: Coachwork by Daniel Girod. Based on a shortened 2CV chassis, with a normal 2CV engine, this is a very well-dressed Duck indeed. Looking like a 2CV only back as far as the windscreen, it has a completely removable hard top, wood-panelled dashboard, chrome trim and luggage rack at the rear.

Above right: Another 2CV version with coachwork by Daniel Girod.

Some specially produced cars such as these retain their 2CV family resemblance; others less so. In the 1950s, the Marquis de Pontac, from Bordeaux was the proud owner of a 2CV based racing car. Some parts of the body were plastic, others aluminium; it could achieve 130km/ hour!

Forty Years On

'Amazing — after 28 years, the Citroën 2CV is to get a facelift. Shame, it doesn't need a facelift. Relax, the Citroën 2CV Charleston is merely a limited edition special, a new paint job, and in character with the car.'

This was how *Autocar* introduced the latest 2CV in 1981; and if their maths left something to be desired — or perhaps they were only counting right-hand drives — their sentiments were entirely correct. They continued: 'It hasn't changed, it doesn't need a facelift like some vain, overweight has-been film star.' The Delage red-and-black Charleston was indeed a limited edition, of 400 cars, which were all snapped up as soon as they were released. Higher priced than the Club, it sported 1930s-style nostalgia which also echoed some of the shapes from earlier in the 2CV history. It sold so well that the edition was continued — limited only by how many could be sold — this time with the round headlights reintroduced and other more minor changes. An alternative colour scheme — yellow and black — was introduced; this time it really was a limited edition — only 27 were imported into Holland for example. Another limited edition, this time in two-tone grey, soon followed. When testing the Charleston, US magazine *Road and Track* commented 'How many cars have had their power output more than tripled and their top speed nearly doubled, while remaining in continuous production, essentially unchanged in structure and appearance, for 37 years? [Many cars] sell for less than a 'new' 2CV6, but how many interesting new friends will they make for you? The Citroën 2CV Charleston registered 7.4 grins per mile on our Smileometer, a new record.'

1981 also saw the release of the James Bond movie *For Your Eyes Only*. It is one of the Duck's most famous film appearances. 007 drives the car down a mountainside in Corfu, hurls it through the olive groves, and makes it leap

Previous pages: Older style Dutch number plates in black, and yellow headlamp bulbs give an extra feeling of 'Frenchness' to this Duck in Utrecht. The car is a lovingly restored 1972 2CV4.

Above: A beautiful white 2CV6 Spécial.

Left: One of the two rarer Charleston versions, in light and dark grey. The nostalgic circle door shape is reminiscent of that of the 1939 prototype.

Above right: The three Charleston versions. Delage red and black was by far the most popular. Originally a special edition of limited number, its production was extended to match demand. The light grey/dark grey and yellow/black options were strictly limited in number. Charlestons are very popular in Holland and England, less so in France. They have the air of sophisticated town cars, rather than that of the practical, down to earth working vehicle which the average plainly painted 2CV projects.

Right: Three Dutch Ducks — birds of a feather.

over a Peugeot. Three cars were used for filming and none of them were written off in the course of the dangerous stunts involved. Indeed, when filming finished, all three were quite drivable. The cars were reinforced and strengthened by the building of a complete frame within the car, and a frame under the floor. When called upon to roll down a bank and then continue driving along, the car did just that. The 602cc engines were replaced with 1015cc units from the Citroën GS. The cars looked like standard 2CVs, but unfortunately they sounded like GSs. The problem was solved by fitting two exhausts, each connected to only two cylinders. One protruded in the normal way, the other did not. An anti-roll bar from the Ami Super, and Kombi shock absorbers at the front, helped the car to stay stable and do its tricks, while still looking like a normal 2CV in front of the cameras.

During the 1980s most of the changes to the 2CV have been superficial. An E (for economy) version of the Spécial was introduced. The 'Dolly' went on sale in Britain in 1985. Its two-colour paintwork was offered in three versions: grey and red, grey and cream, and white and grey. Later came white and green, white and red, and cream and maroon. The Dolly was intended to appeal to a younger car-buying public, and reflected the buoyant mood of the times. On the other side of the Channel, 'France 3', named after a yacht in the America's Cup, was finished in white with blue stripes; a similar car in Britain was called 'Beachcomber'. 'Cocorico', a patriotic car with the colours of the French flag, was sold in France in a limited edition of 1000 in 1986, while in Britain 'Bamboo', which was green, was briefly popular. In Belgium in 1988, 1000 'Perrier' cars in green and white, went on sale.

Citroën's advertising of the 2CV diminished during the 1980s, as it became clear that production would soon cease. During this time, however, a feature was made of the car's quaint looks. It was compared to a snail and, in a now famous advert which has been reproduced as a car sticker, to a tortoise. Four line drawings of the metamorphosis from tortoise to 2CV appear with the heading 'It taught us all we know.' The copy runs: 'It's not all bad being a tortoise. They do live to a very old age. They suffer few mechan-

Previous pages: A Spécial in Brighton.

Left: Black and yellow Spécials, with Charleston. Only 27 yellow and black versions of the Charleston were imported into Holland.

Above: A 1979 2CV6 Spécial. Round headlamps were reintroduced with the Spécial in 1975. The first Spécial was bright yellow, starting a trend for 2CVs in bold, bright colours. A contrast indeed with the days when the 2CV was available only in grey, although yellow wheels did make an appearance in 1953!

Right: 2CV windows have always opened in this way. In the early days there were no catches to hold them open. Before indicators were introduced, quick access for hand signalling purposes was essential. Older 2CVs can often be seen hurtling along a country lane with the bottom halves of the windows flapping wildly.

tell of their life. Some are professionally produced – others are a labour of love, representing years-worth of weekends of work to their owners. There are the artworks on wheels; anything from a standard Duck in a vibrant colour to a complete landscape painting covering every panel. And the cheeky ones: duck stickers, flowers, kites, balloons.

With the closing of the Levellois factory in 1988, production of the 2CV effectively came to an end, although some continued to be assembled abroad, notably in Portugal. At the end of 1984, 35 years after its intro-duction, the 2CV was hailed as 'the cheapest car to run' in France.

Although no longer produced the Duck holds a special place in the hearts of its many fans, whose numbers continue to grow. Driving through rural France, there are still 2CVs to be seen on farms and in vineyards, outside shops and markets in every village. In both Britain and Holland more are to be found in the towns than the country. There are, of course, second-hand 2CVs available. Most of the uniquely painted and coachworked examples have come to their owners in this way. In 1985 *Autocar*, in its 'Buying Secondhand' review, assures us that the 2CV 'stands up to a great deal of neglect and abuse, and carries on gently puttering about its business for many years. It takes a great deal of rust, and ignoring of services, to render a 2CV/Dyane unroadworthy.' But, in case the Duck's reputation or their positive comments have made us over enthusiastic *Autocar* reminds us that 'they are not, however, indestructible.'

From its conception until the end of production, one of the things that has made the 2CV unique is the way in which it has been made *for* its customers. In this it shares a philosophy with many a great sports car. The car was built with regard for a particular set of values, to enhance people's quality of life. In France it is seen as a practical car; abroad it seems quintessentially French, its Gallic charm ranking alongside other typically French things – garlic, baguettes, Pernod and Gauloises. It is not the most successful small car of the century (the durable, but less accommodating VW Beetle wins that accolade), but it is certainly one of the best-loved. The 2CV will soldier on for many years . . . probably at an alarming angle to the road.

ical breakdowns. They have a very poor appetite for consuming petrol. They're not, as we know, the swiftest of creatures. But need we remind you of the story of the tortoise and the hare?'

Some of the most splendid Ducks of the 1980s have been the unique, customized ones, with brilliantly executed coachwork around gleaming mechanics, and layers of beautiful, rich paintwork in amazing colour schemes. Rolls-Royce grilles, removable hoods, running boards, polished chrome, luggage racks, leather seats. Then there are the restored cars; original details, the right grille, sympathetic paint colour, most with a story to

Above left: Hello Dolly! sang the front of the brochure for Citroën's latest special edition 2CV in 1985. In the illustration, a grey and red Dolly wearing long eyelashes on her round headlamps looks alluringly out of the page. Inside, three Dollies sit centre stage in the spotlight – billed as 'The Queens of Show-Biz'. The Dolly was designed to appeal to a younger generation of driver, who needed an inexpensive and frugal car at a time when petrol was very expensive and concern for the environment was growing.

Left: Bamboo, a limited edition in bright green, with a very modern feel.

Above: A yacht called *France 3* gave its name to this special edition 2CV. Part of the profits from the sale of the car went towards the building of the yacht and its participation in the America's Cup races. The same car was available in England, but was called Beachcomber.

Right: Dolly's finishing touch; her name beneath the windscreen.

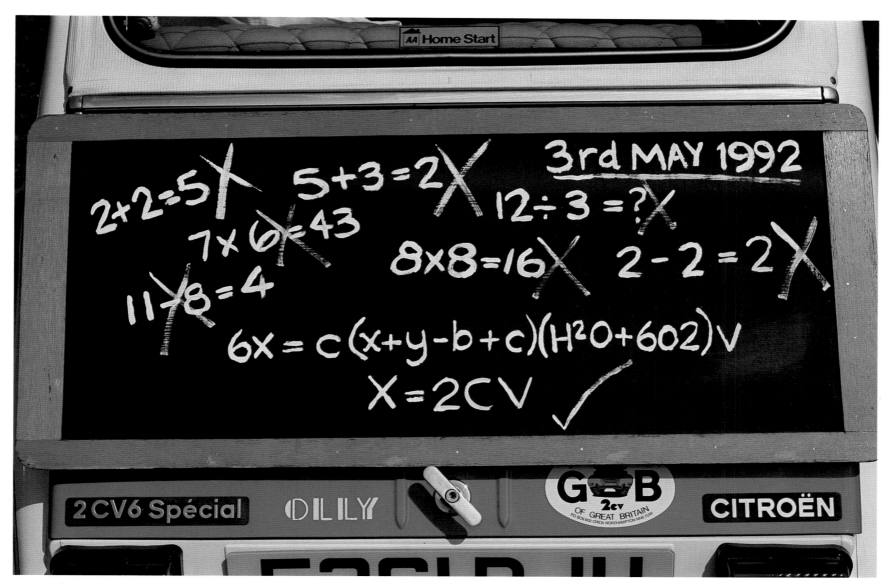

Above left: 2CVs have featured in Tintin cartoons several times; these cartoons have been used as part of Citroën's publicity material. Milou the dog appears on this bootlid without his owner.

Left: Not just a pretty design; the owner of this 2CV is an enthusiastic crew member of a hot-air balloon team.

Above: Nought out of ten for maths, but ten out of ten for style, Olly.

Right: Not a Sahara — the bootlid of a Dolly.

Overleaf, above: A very English character adorns the boot of a very French car.

Overleaf, below: This wonderful bootlid painting is a prime example of just how much time, talent and patience the 2CV enthusiast is prepared to devote to the Duck.

Index

Acknowledgments

Design: David Eldred
Index: Helen Dawson
Production: Veronica Price

The majority of the photographs in this book were taken by David Sparrow. The publishers are grateful to the following for the pictures on the pages noted below:
Neill Bruce/Peter Roberts Collection: 14-15 all 4, 16 both, 26-7 both, 40 below, 53 below.
Citroën: 4-5, 28-9, 30, 32, 33 both, 36, 39 top, 40 below, 44 all 3, 58 top, 73 top, 76 below

The author and photographer would like to thank the following people for their help in preparing this book:

France – Citroën Paris, particularly Mme Agrel Hoeg, Florence Lebottel and Marcel Allard.
Daniel Girod-Roux

The Netherlands – Frans van de Water, Joost Jager, Willem Aal, Martin Punter, Marchel Koops, Paul-Frank Moerman, Bouwen & Susan Scheijgrond, Johan en Joke v.d.Wal, Esther Pangemanen, Lies Linnekamp, Paul van den Berg, Gerard Snÿders, René Vas, Ellen & Henk Bovenkerk, Marcel van Schaik, P J Goverde, Paul Verwey, Hettie Haan, Henk van Wezel, F H Friederich, Peter van Velzen, Annelies Kamerbeek, C P de Haan, M W Goeree, Ton de Graaf, Fam Koolmees, Hans & Loes Monsee.

Britain – Nick Thompson, Steve Hill, Lesley Cooke, Malcolm Blanksby, Jane Dixon, Janice McHardy, David & Marion Lanham, Sarah & Roger Keable, Jennifer Leslie, Jane Tweed, Jeremy Moss, Peter Harper, Trevor Richardson, Jon Colley, Roy Eastwood, Julia Hodgkin, Simon Thomas, Leigh Gooding, David Conway, Thomas Eckered, Carole Stevens, Andrew Minney, Joanna Kelly.

Switzerland – Alfred Gut

We are especially indebted to the following who were good enough to model in our photographs: Gert-Jan Pelt, Tim van Daal, Esther Pangemanen, Marchel & Sandra, Jade Bond, Jenny Irving, Rachel Hollins.

We would like to dedicate the book to CLIVE ABBOTT to thank him for his encouragement and friendship.